KEYSTONE SPECIES

Meet the Animals Key to Ecosystem Health and Biodiversity

WITH HANDS-ON SCIENCE ACTIVITIES FOR KIDS

LAURA PERDEW

ILLUSTRATED BY MICAH RAUCH

More science titles from Nomad Press

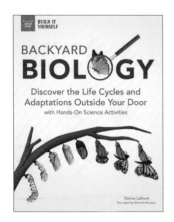

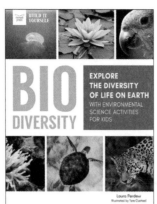

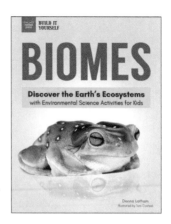

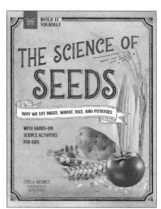

Check out more titles at www.nomadpress.net

Nomad Press

A division of Nomad Communications

10 9 8 7 6 5 4 3 2 1

This book was manufactured by Versa Press, East Peoria, Illinois
October 2024, Job #J24-54945
ISBN Softcover: 978-1-64741-123-7
ISBN Hardcover: 978-1-64741-120-6

Educational Consultant, Marla Conn

Questions regarding the ordering of this book should be addressed to
Nomad Press
PO Box 1036, Norwich, VT 05055
www.nomadpress.net

Printed in the United States.

CONTENTS

Interested in Primary Sources? Look for this icon.

Some of the QR codes in this book link to primary sources that offer firsthand information about the topic. Many photos are considered primary sources because a photograph takes a picture at the moment something happens. Use a smartphone or tablet app to scan the QR code and explore more! You can find a list of the URLs on the Resources page. You can also use the suggested keywords to find other helpful sources.

🔎 keystone species

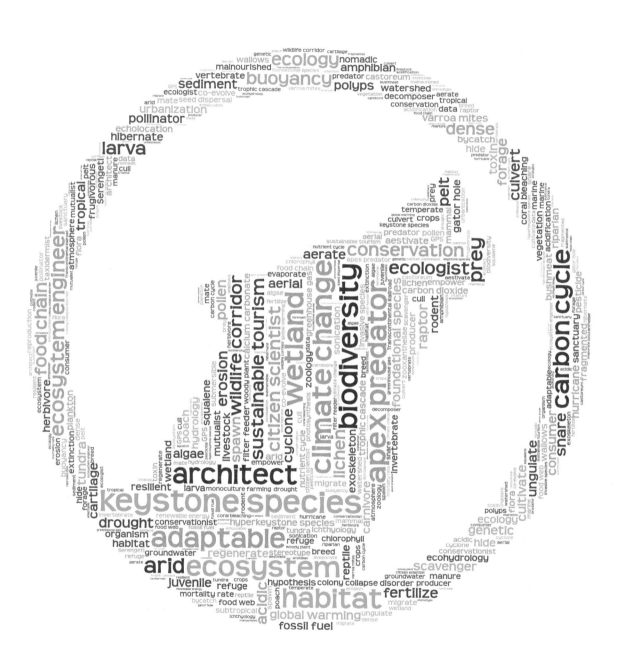

WHAT ARE

KEYSTONE SPECIES?

Imagine an archway made of stone or bricks. At the very top of the arch is a single piece that locks all the other pieces into place. It holds the arch together. The arch would collapse without it. That piece is called the **keystone**.

ESSENTIAL QUESTION

Why is it important to challenge scientific assumptions?

You are probably wondering what an archway has to do with **ecology**. Keep reading!

keystone: a central stone at the top of an arch that locks the whole together. Also, the central part of a system.

ecology: the study of the patterns of relationship between species in an ecosystem.

ecosystem: an interdependent community of living and nonliving things and their environment.

species: a group of organisms that share common traits and can reproduce offspring of their own kind.

organism: any living thing, such as a plant or animal.

keystone species: a species that plays an essential role in an ecosystem and without which the ecosystem would be greatly altered.

ecologist: a scientist who studies the interaction between organisms and their environment.

food chain: a community of plants and animals where each is eaten by another higher up on the chain.

food web: a network of connected food chains.

producer: a part of the food chain that includes plants, which make their food through photosynthesis.

herbivore: an animal that eats only plants.

predator: an animal or plant that kills and eats other animals.

hypothesis: an unproven idea that tries to explain certain facts or observations.

photosynthesis: the process a plant goes through to make its food. The plant uses water and carbon dioxide in the presence of sunlight to make oxygen and sugar.

Now, imagine an **ecosystem**. Within every ecosystem in the world, there are living and nonliving things. Together, they create a community. In that community, all the plants and animals have roles to play to keep the ecosystem healthy.

Yet some **species** are more important than others—they have the same role in their ecosystems that a keystone has in an arch. Without these **organisms**, the ecosystem would collapse. That is why they are called **keystone species**.

DISCOVERY!

Ecologists are scientists who study the relationships between organisms and their environment within an ecosystem. Part of their job is to study **food chains** and **food webs**.

Before the 1960s, scientists thought that the number of **producers** in an ecosystem limited the number of **herbivores**. And, in turn, the number of herbivores limited how many **predators** there were. In other words, they thought everything in the ecosystem was regulated by how much food was available, starting at the *bottom* of the food chain.

But some scientists wondered: Why didn't the herbivores just devour all the plants? Why were any plants left in the ecosystem?

Scientists came up with a new **hypothesis**. They proposed that the number of herbivores was controlled by the number of producers *and* by the number of predators. This was a switch from what scientists had assumed, that predators didn't play any significant role in the overall ecosystem.

The idea that predators helped regulate herbivore populations was an entirely new way to think of food webs. After all, how could predators help to keep the world green?

The energy being passed around in a food web originally comes from the sun. Through photosynthesis, green plants get their energy from the sun. The animals eating those plants are benefitting from the sun's energy, too.

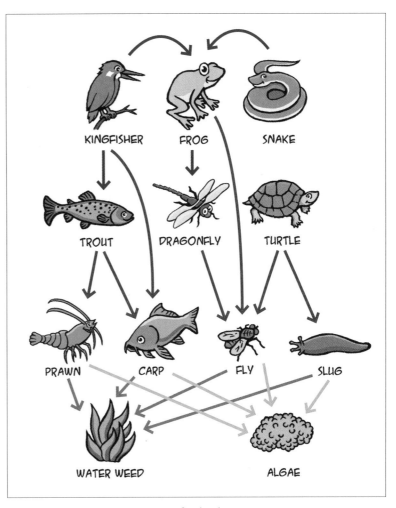

A food web

Scientists faced a problem: How could they run a controlled experiment on a natural ecosystem? Enter Robert Paine (1933–2016), a zoology professor at the University of Washington. In the early 1960s, he wanted to find a system he could control and manipulate to test the hypothesis. He discovered the tidepools on the Pacific Coast of Washington—each one was its own tiny ecosystem with more than a dozen species living there. It was the perfect place to run the experiment.

KEYSTONE SPECIES

WORDS TO KNOW

filter feeder: an animal that gets its food by filtering food particles or tiny living things from water.

scavenger: an animal, bird, or insect that eats rotting food or animals that are already dead.

algae: a plant-like organism that lives in water and grows by converting energy from the sun into food.

carnivorous: describes a carnivore, a plant or animal that eats only animals.

data: facts and observations about something.

Paine started by observing and recording all of the species that lived in the tidepools. There were **filter feeders** and **scavengers** and **algae** and other plants. At the very top of the food chain was a **carnivorous** starfish.

To see what would happen to the ecosystem without its top predator, Paine removed the starfish from one tidepool. He left the starfish in the other tidepools. Any time a starfish reappeared in the experimental tidepool, it was removed.

Within 18 months, that tidepool had changed. The number of other species had dropped. After eight years, the tidepool contained only a single organism—mussels.

What happened? When starfish were present, they kept the mussels from taking over. Without the top predator, the mussels pushed out all other species.

Scientist Spotlight: Bob Paine

Robert Paine and the starfish changed the field of ecology forever. Before Paine, the field of ecology was mostly about describing patterns in nature. He changed it to one that included experiments and **data**. As a boy, Paine was always interested in nature. He spent much of his youth exploring the woods. In an interview, Paine said, "All my early childhood memories involve biology." That passion eventually led him to the Pacific Northwest. He was a professor at the University of Washington for decades. That's where he discovered the ecosystems of the tidepools. Throughout his life, he continued to do research in the field. He also mentored the next generation of ecologists.

Watch this short video about Bob Paine and his work. Why was his discovery of tidepools as complete ecosystems so important?

🔎 PBS keystone species Paine

Tidal pools in the U.S. state of Washington

A NEW WAY OF THINKING

Paine's discovery changed how we understand ecosystems and food webs. It was groundbreaking! Paine coined the term "keystone species." These species play an important role in their environment. Removing a keystone species from an ecosystem has enormous impact. Its removal causes the entire system to collapse, just like a keystone in an arch.

Paine did other experiments, too. He found that not all species have such a deep impact on their environment as keystone species.

Use the interactive map or the species tiles to discover various keystone species around the world. How do some of these keystone species affect humans in the region?

Media HHMI keystone map

PS

KEYSTONE SPECIES

Keystone species maintain **biodiversity** in an ecosystem. They help determine which other species are in that ecosystem. They also affect how many of each species are there. Plus, no other species can take over the role of a keystone species if they disappear.

When a keystone species does disappear, ecosystems experience a **trophic cascade**. This means that after the keystone species is gone, the effects cascade throughout the whole ecosystem. Every species on every level of the food chain is affected. Some species are pushed out. Others take over.

This is especially concerning because the greater the biodiversity in an ecosystem, the stronger that ecosystem is. And even though not all species have a keystone role, biodiversity keeps ecosystems healthier and more **resilient**.

Trophic cascades have occurred throughout Earth's history. They happen due to species loss, volcanic eruptions, severe weather events, and other ecosystem changes.

The Scientific Method

A scientific method worksheet is a useful tool for keeping your ideas and observations organized. The scientific method is the process scientists use to ask and answer questions. Use a notebook as a science journal to make a scientific method worksheet for each experiment you do.

Question: What are we trying to find out? What problem are we trying to solve?
Research: What is already known about this topic?
Hypothesis: What do we think the answer will be?
Equipment: What supplies are we using?
Method: What procedure are we following?
Results: What happened and why?

Species Spotlight: Purple Starfish

The starfish Robert Paine studied were purple starfish (*Pisaster ochraceous*). They are five-armed **invertebrates** that are ruthless, carnivorous predators. They eat snails, barnacles, mussels, limpets, and even crabs. Yet starfish do not have teeth or jaws. To eat, the starfish pries open shells with its arms. Then, the starfish pushes its stomach out of its mouth. Not only that, it pushes its stomach into the **prey's** shell. It digests its prey before swallowing. Wow!

If this isn't weird enough, starfish can **regenerate** an arm if they lose one. This is important because they use those arms for eating and to move around. Also, starfish do not have a brain. Instead, they have a simple nervous system. It connects with nerves that extend down each arm and signals them to move.

OTHER KEYSTONE SPECIES

After Paine made his great discovery, other biologists conducted more research. They found that keystone species are part of all major ecosystems. Forests, deserts, oceans, **tundra**, grasslands, and **wetlands** all have keystone species. They are also found all over the world at every level of food chains.

Use the American Museum of Natural History's website to learn more about biodiversity and why it's important. What different kinds of species live in your area?

🔍 AMNH what is biodiversity

KEYSTONE SPECIES

WORDS TO KNOW

ecosystem engineer: a species that greatly alters an ecosystem by creating, modifying, maintaining, or destroying it.

mutualists: two or more species in an ecosystem that interact in such a way that both benefit.

foundational species: a species that provides the base on which an entire ecosystem is built.

hyperkeystone species: a species that can have an ecological impact on the entire planet.

conservationist: a person who works to preserve nature.

Scientists further identified several types of keystone species. Predators are one type. Other types of keystone species are **ecosystem engineers**, **mutualists**, herbivores, and **foundational species**. Plants can even be keystone species!

Some keystone species are huge, such as elephants. And some are tiny. It might be hard to believe that tiny organisms can affect entire ecosystems. But they do! Some of the tiniest keystone species are bees (which we'll talk about more in Chapter 6) and krill.

Krill are some of the smallest ocean animals. But they are the base of the marine food chain. They are an important source of food for some of the ocean's largest animals, such as whales. Without krill, many marine animals would be very hungry.

Paine's next study with fellow scientist Jim Estes found that sea otters are another keystone species.

Throughout the book, we'll also take a look at the role of one other species: humans. Many years after his experiment in the tidepools, Paine considered the role of humans in the world. He saw how humans directly and indirectly affect all ecosystems and species. Thus he coined another term: **hyperkeystone species**.

Essential Questions

Each chapter of this book begins with an essential question to help guide your exploration of keystone species. Keep the question in your mind as you read the chapter. At the end of each chapter, use your science journal to record your thoughts and answers.

ESSENTIAL QUESTION

Why is it important to challenge scientific assumptions?

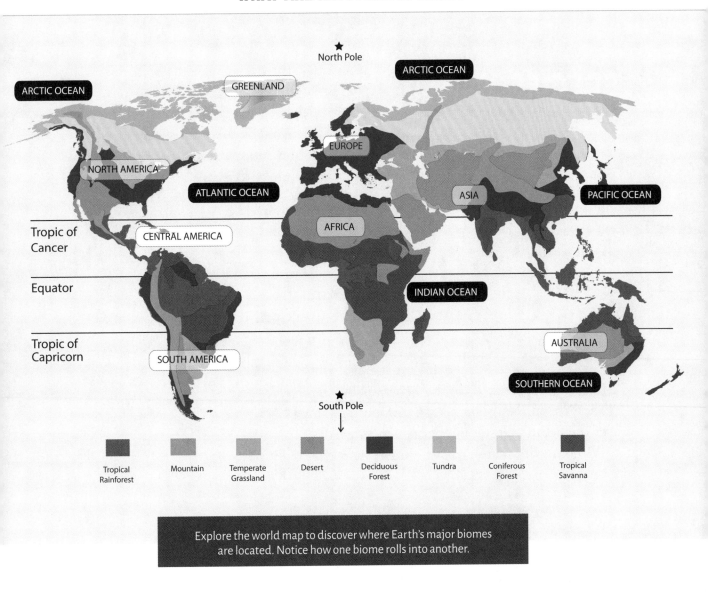

Tropical Rainforest | Mountain | Temperate Grassland | Desert | Deciduous Forest | Tundra | Coniferous Forest | Tropical Savanna

Explore the world map to discover where Earth's major biomes are located. Notice how one biome rolls into another.

As a hyperkeystone species, humans have a huge ecological impact that is felt everywhere on the planet. Can you think of some ways humans change the natural world?

In this book, you'll meet keystone species of all kinds and discover the remarkable roles they play in their ecosystems. You'll learn about threats to these species. You'll also meet the scientists and **conservationists** working to protect them. Prepare to be amazed!

TEXT TO **WORLD**

What are some keystone species where you live?

MAKE A
SPECIES MAP

IDEAS FOR SUPPLIES

- note cards
- writing utensil
- research materials (books or internet)

You will meet a lot of scientists and conservationists in this book. Their work can include creating maps that show the species living in an area. This information tells them which animals or plants are found in different places and the number of each species. It also helps them determine places that need to be protected. Creating your own species map will reveal the species that live near you.

> **Select a natural area you want to map.** This could be a yard, garden, park, or forest. Pick an area that's the size of a basketball court or smaller.

> **Draw a map of the area.** Include all important features of the area, such as buildings, sidewalks, and streets. Add a title, map key, and compass.

> **Start your observation.** You may need to sit quietly and wait for animals. Or you may want to walk around. Binoculars and a magnifying glass can be helpful. When looking for insects, be sure to get up close to plants and trees. Look under rocks and logs.

> **Add all the species you see to your map.** Include plants, flowers, bushes. Add birds, insects, and other animals. Put the species on the map in the location you observed them in. If you see more than one of certain species, record it.

> **Trees and flowers can be tricky!** Ask an adult to help you identify any species you don't recognize.

* How many different species did you observe?

* Was there one part of your map that had more species?

* Did you observe anything that surprised you?

* What did you learn about your area?

Consider This!

Using the information you collected, go online and research the species you observed. Are these species native to your area? Are any of them rare? Are any of them **migrating**? Consider doing your species map at a different time of year. Predict which animals you will see again and which you might not see.

Species Spotlight: Saguaro Cacti

The saguaro cactus is a plant. It is also a keystone species. These giants are found in the **arid**, rocky Sonoran Desert that spans parts of Arizona, California, and Mexico. They can be as tall as 50 feet and 10 feet around. Saguaro cacti live up to 200 years. During their lifetime, these cacti are part hotel, part buffet, and part water storage tank. They provide food and shelter for dozens of animals and insects. Birds such as Gila woodpeckers dig nest holes into the soft, fleshy part of the cactus. After they've moved out, other birds will move in and use the nest holes!

When the saguaro's flowers bloom, they provide nectar and pollen for bats, birds, and insects. The fruit that ripens provides **nutrients** and moisture for desert animals. In especially dry times, some animals such as jackrabbits will even eat the flesh of the cactus for moisture.

WORDS TO KNOW

migrate: to move from one environment to another when seasons change.

arid: very dry, receiving little rain.

nutrients: substances in food, water, and soil that living things need to live and grow.

Chapter 1

SHAKING UP

SHARKS

Sharks and purple starfish—not a lot in common, right? Purple starfish are five-armed invertebrates. And, despite their names, they are not fish! On the other hand, sharks are fish. They have fins and breathe through gills, like all fish. They are **vertebrates** but have skeletons made of **cartilage**, not bone, unlike most fish.

ESSENTIAL QUESTION

How can understanding sharks help protect them?

What do they have in common? Both are keystone species—and both are **apex predators**.

Sharks seem much scarier than starfish, though. And they have a bad reputation! Among a school of fish, sharks seem like bullies. They are sharp-toothed, fierce, and terrifying.

As predators, sharks are doing what they need to do to survive. Yet their fearsome reputation may keep us from appreciating the important role they play in **marine** ecosystems.

Sharks are found in oceans all over the world, in many different marine **habitats**. They lurk near coral reefs, swim out in deep open water, and even dive under Arctic ice.

Sharks come in many sizes. Some species, such as the dwarf lantern shark, are small—roughly the size of a human hand! Whale sharks are the largest species and can grow almost 40 feet long. That's the length of a full-sized school bus! The smaller species feed on tiny organisms such as **plankton**. Larger sharks eat seals and rays. But the biggest species—whale sharks—feed mostly on plankton, small fish, and squid.

The world's oceans are home to more than 500 different species of sharks.

WORDS TO KNOW

vertebrate: an animal with a backbone.

cartilage: tough, fibrous connective tissue. Our ears and nose are made of cartilage.

apex predator: a species at the top of the food chain with no natural predators of its own.

marine: having to do with the ocean.

habitat: a plant's or animal's home, which supplies it with food, water, and shelter.

plankton: tiny organisms floating in the ocean.

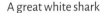

A great white shark

WORDS TO KNOW

ichthyology: the study of fish.

PhD: doctor of philosophy, the highest degree in an area of study given by a college or university.

zoology: the study of animals.

submersible: a boat that is designed to go completely underwater.

erosion: the gradual wearing away of sand, soil, or rock by water or wind.

carbon dioxide (CO_2): a colorless, odorless gas. Humans and animals exhale this gas while plants absorb it. It is also a byproduct of burning fossil fuels.

greenhouse gas: a gas in the atmosphere that traps heat. We need some greenhouse gases, but too many trap too much heat and contribute to global warming.

atmosphere: the layer of gases around the earth.

ROLE OF SHARKS

A shark's job in the ocean is like that of the starfish in the tide pools. Sharks hunt and eat prey. Most sharks are apex predators at the top of the food chain. As they hunt, they keep the populations of their prey in check, which keeps ocean food webs balanced.

> Watch this video to learn about the amazing physical features of sharks. Why do you think sharks are both feared and admired?
>
> ⌕ TedEd sharks Thys

For example, many sharks eat mid-sized fish that prey on herbivorous fish. Those herbivores eat plants and algae. By eating algae that harm coral, the herbivorous fish keep the coral healthy. Without sharks, those predatory fish take over and eat herbivorous fish, which means the coral reefs suffer without any fish left to eat the algae.

In addition, sharks prey on unhealthy and injured animals. By doing so, sharks remove the weakest animals, which allows the healthiest ones to reproduce.

Coral that's been killed by algae

Scientist Spotlight: Eugenie Clark

As a child, Eugenie Clark (1922–2015) was fascinated by fish. That passion led her to study **ichthyology** in college and then earn a **PhD** in **zoology**. Clark went diving all over the world using scuba gear and **submersibles** to study marine animals, including sharks. Clark devoted her life to studying sharks in the wild and to teaching others about them—she wanted to change how people thought of them. Her contributions to shark science earned her the nickname the "Shark Lady."

Watch this short video to learn more about Clark's life and contributions to shark science. Did she face extra challenges as a woman working in a scientific field populated mostly by men?

🔎 Visit Cayman Islands Eugenie Clark

In some habitats, sharks promote the growth of seagrass. For example, tiger sharks prowl shallow waters near seagrass meadows looking for prey such as birds, turtles, and stingrays. When a shark is nearby, creatures that forage on the seagrass are scared off. When sharks limit how much time the grazers spend in an area, they prevent overgrazing. More seagrass can grow and help prevent **erosion** by holding sand in place and slowing down incoming waves. Sharks are considered climate heroes for supporting seagrass growth.

Great white sharks grow to about half the length of whale sharks, or 20 feet. The largest ones weigh about 4,500 pounds.

WHAT ABOUT CLIMATE CHANGE?

Wait—sharks are climate heroes? Yes! **Carbon dioxide (CO$_2$)** is a **greenhouse gas** that is important to life on Earth. Greenhouse gases trap heat in the **atmosphere**. They work like a blanket, keeping the heat from the sun in our atmosphere. Without the gases, that heat would escape and Earth would be so cold that nothing could live here.

WORDS TO KNOW

fossil fuel: a natural fuel that formed long ago from the remains of living organisms. Coal, oil, and natural gas are fossil fuels.

climate change: a change in long-term weather patterns, which can happen through natural or manmade processes.

global warming: an increase in the average temperature of the earth's atmosphere, enough to cause climate change.

carbon cycle: the movement of carbon through ecosystems.

fossil: the remains of any living thing, including animals and plants, that have been preserved in rock.

However, we burn **fossil fuels** such as gas and oil to make energy to power our homes, cities, and vehicles. Burning fossil fuels emits greenhouse gases, and too much of those greenhouse gases stay in the atmosphere. The results are **climate change** and **global warming**. As we burn more fossil fuels, temperatures on Earth will continue to rise.

One way to slow or stop climate change is to decrease the use of fossil fuels. Another way is to capture and store the carbon before it's released into the atmosphere as carbon dioxide.

Learn more about the issues facing planet Earth at NASA's website developed specifically for kids. What can you do to help prevent climate change?

🔎 Climate Kids NASA

Species Spotlight: Blue Crab

In Chesapeake Bay, the blue crab is a keystone species. This crab is both predator and prey. The larvae of blue crabs are food for menhaden fish and oysters. Young crabs and adults are important prey for several species of fish, birds, sea turtles, and sharks.

As a predator, blue crabs are not picky eaters. They even eat other blue crabs! They also prey on oysters, clams, fish, and snails. Their hunger for snails plays a very important role—in areas without blue crabs, periwinkle snails devour marsh grasses. Without the grasses, the ecosystem turns into a barren mudflat. However, in areas where there are blue crabs, the snail population is regulated. That helps to maintain a healthy, balanced salt marsh ecosystem.

Seagrass doing its job to absorb carbon—helped by sharks!

Sharks lived in Earth's oceans long before the time of the dinosaurs. Fossils show that sharks have been around for more than 400 million years.

Rocks, soil, plants, and the ocean naturally absorb carbon as part of the **carbon cycle**.

This is where sharks and other animals come in! When keystone species are present and healthy in an ecosystem, that ecosystem has greater biodiversity and includes more plants and trees. As a result, more carbon can be stored there.

As we learned, sharks promote seagrass growth. And seagrass meadows absorb carbon from the atmosphere, which helps fight climate change. More sharks mean greater carbon storage. Their presence not only keeps the ecosystem healthy and balanced, it also has much wider environmental benefits.

WHO HUNTS SHARKS?

Sharks may be apex predators, but they do have one enemy: humans. People hunt sharks for their meat, fins, and other parts. Overfishing has led to a 70-percent decline in shark populations since 1970.

On the Smithsonian's ocean website about sharks, scroll down to the very bottom of the page to watch the video. How does this map show a change in attitude toward sharks from 1980 to 2014? Please note that the web page includes graphic images of dead sharks.

🔍 Smithsonian sharks rays

KEYSTONE SPECIES

WORDS TO KNOW

squalene: a natural oil found in sharks and some plants that people use in medicine, cosmetics, and cleansers.

bycatch: marine species caught accidentally in a net while fishing for other species.

extinction: the death of an entire species so that it no longer exists.

The fins are one of the most valuable parts of sharks. In Asia, shark fin soup is popular. Some people believe the soup has many health benefits, but science does not back that belief.

Sharks are also targeted for an oil called **squalene**, which is found in their liver. People use squalene in medicines, lotions, make-up, cleansers, and more. Many sharks are hunted only for squalene, and the rest of the shark is discarded.

Approximately 100 million sharks are caught as **bycatch** every year. When fishermen are trying to catch other species, sharks can also get caught in their nets. New hook and fishing line designs can improve sharks' chances for escape and survival.

Shark populations are also at risk because they grow slowly. Plus, they take a long time to reproduce and have few offspring at a time. As a result, sharks are killed faster than they reproduce. Almost one-third of shark species are at risk of **extinction**.

In 2009, the small Pacific-island nation of Palau was the first to create a shark sanctuary. Shark fishing is illegal in the 240,000-square-mile sanctuary.

Gill nets hanging in the ocean. This method of fishing traps a lot of bycatch.

CONSERVATION IN ACTION

Across the globe, people are working to protect sharks. Many organizations push for regulations to protect sharks and their habitats. They raise money and influence lawmakers.

One effort resulted in a fishing ban around Australia's Ashmore Reef in 2008. By 2016, the shark population there had increased by more than 25 percent. Once the sharks were back, they kept the population of mid-sized predator fish in check.

Take a look at this infographic about the importance of sharks. What can we do to help prevent shark populations from shrinking?

🔎 Climate Kids NASA

That led to an increase in the number of herbivorous fish. The herbivorous fish grazed on algae that can smother the corals that make up the reef. Thanks to the return of sharks, the reef is healthy once again.

KEYSTONE SPECIES

In the United States, the Shark Finning Prohibition Act was signed in 2000. Under the law, fishermen cannot take only the fin of a shark. The National Marine Fisheries Service uses research and data to manage shark populations and legal fishing. In addition, many species of shark are listed under the Endangered Species Act. People cannot hurt, chase, harass, kill, or capture species on this list.

Plant-based squalene is another way to protect sharks. Rice bran, olives, and wheat germ all contain the oil that's in high demand. A 2015 study showed that more than 80 percent of all squalene in the United States and Europe was from non-animal sources. That's good news for sharks!

International cooperation and management are also key to shark **conservation**. Sharks freely roam the ocean and don't know when they've crossed from one country's waters to another's. Many of these international efforts focus on monitoring the international trade of wild animals so that their populations remain **sustainable**.

Having fish for dinner? Use the Monterey Bay Aquarium's Seafood Watch website to make informed choices about the seafood you eat. How do our small personal choices affect the larger world?

🔎 seafood watch

A tagged whale shark in Australia. Scientists can track the shark's movements and learn about its life and habitat.

*TEXT TO **WORLD***

Have you seen movies or read books about sharks? How are they often portrayed?

Organizations Protecting Sharks

Several organizations work to conserve shark populations worldwide. Look at the information on their websites. How can you become a part of the solution?

› **Shark Conservation Fund:** sharkconservationfund.org

› **Shark Research Institute:** sharks.org

› **Shark Specialist Group** (part of the International Union for Conservation of Nature): iucnssg.org

No matter where you live or how old you are, you can help protect sharks! Here are some tips.

• Check the ingredients list! Avoid buying products such as shark fin soup. If something contains squalene, make sure it's plant-based.

• If you go on a tour to see sharks or other marine **mammals**, choose the tour company carefully. Be sure the company supports protected areas and looks out for the well-being of sharks.

Watch this video about what might happen if sharks disappeared. Why is a living shark worth more than a dead shark? How can knowing more about sharks help us conquer our fear of them?

🔎 Environmental Humanities great white shark

• Spread the word! Tell everyone you know about what is happening to sharks and how important they are to our oceans.

• You can also support groups that help sharks or write letters to government officials to encourage them to protect sharks.

ESSENTIAL QUESTION

How can understanding sharks help protect them?

Now, let's move up on land to learn about another keystone species that sometimes has a sinister reputation—gray wolves!

HOW DO
SHARKS STAY AFLOAT?

IDEAS FOR SUPPLIES

- bucket or sink (with a plug)
- water
- 2 small water bottles or Ziploc bags
- vegetable oil
- science journal

Most fish have a swim bladder, which is an organ filled with gases, including oxygen. Fish use the bladder to control their **buoyancy**. Like a balloon filled with helium in the air, the swim bladder helps fish stay afloat or descend deeper into the water. When they want to rise, fish fill the bladder. When they want to descend, they expel the gas.

Sharks don't have a swim bladder! How do they stay afloat? The oil in their liver helps make them buoyant. Another factor helping sharks stay afloat is the fact they have cartilage, not bones. Cartilage is lighter than bone. Plus, their fins and tails keep sharks moving constantly. Make a model to observe how sharks float.

> Fill the bucket or sink with water.

> Fill one water bottle with oil and one with water, so each bottle has the same amount of liquid in it. Tighten the lids on the bottles. The bottles represent sharks.

> Make a prediction— will the bottles sink or float? Write your hypothesis in your science journal.

> Place the bottle with water in the bucket or sink. Does it stay afloat or sink?

> Place the bottle with oil in the bucket or sink. Does it stay afloat or sink?

> Based on this experiment, which is more **dense**, oil or water?

Try This

Try filling your "shark" water bottle with different kinds of oil. Fill to the same level every time and place in the bucket or sink. Does the type of oil affect the buoyancy? You can also redo the experiment and fill the sink or bucket with liquids other than water. How does the type of liquid affect the buoyancy of your shark? Why do you think this is?

WORDS TO KNOW

buoyancy: inclined to stay afloat.

dense: how tightly the matter in an object is packed.

PROFILE OF THE
WORLD'S SHARKS

IDEAS FOR SUPPLIES

- research materials (books or internet)
- science journal
- colored pencils

Sharks live in a variety of marine habitats in oceans around the world. Hundreds of species come in many different shapes and sizes. Educating people about different types of sharks is key to protecting them!

❯ Find information on 10 to 15 of the world's most well-known species of shark or ones that catch your attention.

❯ Create a short profile of each species. Record its name, the ocean it lives in, its marine habitat, its size and color, what it eats, and any other interesting information.

❯ Draw a thumbnail sketch of each species or print out a photograph.

❯ Create a poster to educate people about different species of sharks.

Try This

Create a book or poster of shark superlatives. Research the world's smallest shark—and the largest. Which sharks live the longest? Which sharks are the most unusual shape or color? Get creative with your superlatives!

Sharks in Hawaii

Western culture sees sharks as fearsome predators. In Hawaiian culture, however, sharks—called *manō*—are important and respected. One Hawaiian legend describes how sharks guided the first people across the ocean to the Hawaiian Islands. Native Hawaiians also believe certain sharks, called *'aumakua*, are the spirits of dead relatives. Not all sharks are 'aumakua, but the 'aumakua are thought to provide wisdom and protection to a family. These sharks are often fed and cared for across generations.

Although some Hawaiian communities have hunted sharks for food, they used all the parts of the shark, including their skin and teeth. Can you think of other species that have played large roles in other cultures?

DO PLANTS
REDUCE EROSION?

In some places, sharks on the hunt scare other species out of seagrass meadows and prevent the meadows from being overgrazed. The seagrass can grow healthily and help prevent erosion. See for yourself!

❯ Poke holes in the bottom of the pans for drainage. Fill both bread pans with soil. Plant the seeds closely together in one pan. Do not plant any seeds in the other pan.

❯ **Place the pan with the seeds near a sunny window with something underneath the pan to catch water.** Water the seeds.

❯ **When the plants are 3 to 4 inches tall, remove the pan from the window.** Take both bread pans outside. On each pan, cut along the corners of one short end so the side can fold down. Place an object 1 to 2 inches tall underneath the non-cut side of both bread pans. The pans should be at an angle with the cut, open end down.

❯ **Use your watering can to make it "rain" gently on both bread pans and give both pans the same amount of water.** Do this until your watering can is empty.

❯ **What do you observe?** Did soil wash out of both pans? Based on your experiment, did the plants help to reduce erosion? How is this similar or different from plants in the real world?

IDEAS FOR SUPPLIES

- 2 foil bread loaf pans
- enough soil to fill both pans
- fast-growing seeds such as beans, radishes, or grass
- a sunny window for the plants
- a watering can with a rain spout

Try This

Do the experiment again in several pans with different seeds and space them at different distances. You can also try using different types of soil, rock, or sand.

Chapter 2

GEARING UP FOR

GRAY WOLVES

Like sharks, wolves are an apex predator with a not-so-great reputation. They are the evil villains of fairy tales and stories, where their sharp teeth create the image of a big, bad character. But like sharks, wolves do not hunt to be mean. They hunt because they are **carnivores** and need to eat to survive. And their hunting is key to the health of their ecosystem. Without wolves, ecosystems change greatly—wolves are a keystone species.

Gray wolves live in North America, Europe, and Asia in a variety of habitats such as **temperate** forests, tundra, grasslands, and deserts. Their ability to thrive in diverse habitats shows how **adaptable** they are.

But no matter where they live, their main prey is hooved animals. That includes elk, deer, moose, and other **ungulates**.

ESSENTIAL QUESTION

How did the disappearance of wolves in Yellowstone National Park affect its ecosystem?

KEYSTONE SPECIES

ON THE HUNT

While wolves are often villains in fiction, in real life they are nature's heroes. Their hunting keeps the populations of their prey in balance, along with the animals and plants that their prey eat. When wolves are removed from an ecosystem, the entire food web is impacted. A trophic cascade occurs.

What does this mean? Wolves prey on elk, deer, and other ungulates. Without wolves to hunt them, the population of these animals increases. Most ungulates are herbivores. When their numbers increase, they eat more shrubs, grasses, and young trees. As time passes, the ungulates overgraze the vegetation. Also, some trees such as willows or aspen cannot grow to full size. Without these trees, birds and other mammals have no habitat and smaller animals don't have vegetation to hide in for safety. Even grizzly bears are affected because there are fewer berries to go around. Plus, **pollinators** have fewer flowers to visit.

River and stream ecosystems are also affected when wolves disappear. When wolves are present, ungulates tend to avoid spending much time in the open, where they are easy targets for a hungry wolf pack.

But, without wolves around, the ungulates can graze along the water's edge without fear of being hunted. Not only do they devour the vegetation along the water that prevents stream erosion, but their hooves also destroy the banks. Dirt and other **sediment** cloud the water and affect fish populations. No vegetation along the water's edge means no shade. This raises water temperatures, which directly impacts trout, which need cooler water to thrive.

Every wolf has its own unique howl. Howling is the way wolves communicate with pack members and with rivals.

Beavers also need the vegetation typically found along streams and riverbanks to build their dams. The dams create ponds and habitat for countless other species. Without the vegetation they need, beavers disappear. And, yes, beavers are a keystone species, too! We'll get to them in the next chapter.

Scientist Spotlight: Doug Smith

Doug Smith's interest in wolves began in childhood. He wrote letters to wolf biologists, volunteered at a local wolf center, and later spent several summers in Isle Royale National Park assisting with research.

During the early 1990s, Smith was hired to reintroduce wolves to Yellowstone. He and others then began to monitor the wolves using field observations, radio collars, and **aerial** tracking. They discovered much about the social structure of wolf packs and wolves' role as a keystone species. The Yellowstone Wolf Restoration Project has become the world's leading wolf research program.

Watch some short National Park Service videos with Doug Smith answering questions about wolves. Why is it important to understand complex ecosystems?

Doug Smith NPS

KEYSTONE SPECIES

Another way wolves help the ecosystem is that they hunt the weakest and sickest animals. Removing them from the herd allows the strongest animals to survive and reproduce and keeps diseases from spreading

Like sharks, wolves are climate heroes. When wolves are present in their natural ecosystem, more trees and plants can grow and absorb carbon. More wolves mean greater carbon storage. Wolves offer a natural way to fight climate change!

Wolves are family animals and the most social of all carnivores. They live and hunt in packs led by an alpha female and male.

THREATS FACED BY WOLVES

As with many other apex predators, the wolves' only threat is humans. Before the arrival of European settlers, wolves lived throughout much of North America, existing in harmony with Native Americans. As settlers moved across the continent, they wiped out the wolves' prey, such as bison and deer. Without food, hungry wolves preyed on **livestock**. A wolf must eat!

Family Structure of a Wolf Pack

Wolves are intelligent and social animals. They live in packs of 4 to 10 wolves that consist of a **mating** pair and their offspring. The pair usually mates for life. Some larger packs might also include grandparents, aunts, and uncles. Young wolves stay with their birth pack until the age of two or three.

Wolf packs live within and defend an established territory that can cover hundreds of square miles. Wolf packs hunt together in a coordinated group effort. All adults in the pack help look out for, feed, and teach the pups. The wolves communicate with each other by howling, barking, whining, and using body language.

Settlers saw wolves as a threat to their safety and to the development of the country. They hated, feared, hunted, and poisoned wolves throughout the 1800s and into the early 1900s. People known as "wolfers" were hired to get rid of wolves. Even the U.S. government backed wolf controls.

All our pet dogs of today are descended from wolves.

At the time, scientists were still learning about how ecosystems work and didn't know how everything was connected. They didn't understand or respect the role of wolves in the ecosystem. The last wolf in Yellowstone National Park was killed in 1926, and by the 1930s, wolves were almost eliminated in the rest of the United States.

CONSERVATION EFFORTS

The fate of wolves finally changed during the second half of the twentieth century when scientists began to understand how ecosystems function and that each species plays an important role. And, of course, Robert Paine made his breakthrough discovery of keystone species in the 1960s. With that knowledge, attitudes shifted and government policies changed.

A key moment for wolves came with the passage of the Endangered Species Act in 1973. Gray wolves were on the list of endangered animals so people could not hunt or harm them. Equally importantly, government agencies were required to create plans to restore wolf populations to their native ecosystems.

As early as the 1940s, scientist Aldo Leopold (1887–1948) recommended that wolves be returned to Yellowstone. He is regarded as the father of wildlife ecology.

One of the most famous examples of wolf conservation happened at Yellowstone National Park. When scientists discussed the reintroduction of wolves to native habitats, the question was always: where? Many people still hated and feared wolves. And wolves were still predators that need to hunt to survive.

Species Spotlight: Australian Dingo

Far from Yellowstone National Park, another canine keystone species has a story similar to that of gray wolves. Like the wolves, the Australian dingo is an apex predator. Although not native to Australia, they have been there for almost 5,000 years and today play a keystone role in the ecosystem. Yet they are also feared and despised by many.

Dingoes are found across Australia in a variety of habitats, including forests, grasslands, tropical areas, and deserts. Their presence in these ecosystems helps keep the population of other species in check. Dingoes hunt other carnivores in the food web, such as fox. They also prey on a variety of herbivores. As with the wolf, this predation affects the entire ecosystem, keeping it balanced. And that balance increases biodiversity.

A gray wolf and a bison at Yellowstone National Park

Yellowstone is a vast wilderness with few people. Its ecosystem had suffered without its apex predator. The elk population had soared without wolves, causing the park to become overgrazed by all those hungry herbivores. The ecosystem was out of balance. So, why not bring wolves back to Yellowstone?

Armed with clear scientific knowledge, the Park Service developed a plan of action. In 1995 and 1996, they reintroduced 31 gray wolves to Yellowstone. For the first time in decades, the top predator roamed free in the park.

Watch this video about wolves and their history in the United States. How did human movement across the country affect the wolves?

Nat Geo wolves 101

In much the same way that tidal pools became an ecosystem laboratory for Robert Paine, Yellowstone became a natural laboratory. Scientists track and closely monitor the wolves in Yellowstone to see how different species affect each other.

KEYSTONE SPECIES

WORDS TO KNOW

stereotype: an overly simple picture or opinion of a person, group, animal, or thing.

Evidence shows that wolves have decreased elk populations. Biodiversity has increased in many parts of the park. Understanding the effects of the wolves is ongoing since the Yellowstone ecosystem is complex.

Other efforts to reintroduce wolves to wilderness areas are underway.

Watch scientists ask and answer questions about the relationship between predators and prey in Washington state. Why is it important to understand the predator-prey relationship in areas where people live and recreate?

🔎 WA gray wolf influence

Some people still despise wolves and think they are a threat to people and livestock. In response, conservation groups have created programs to pay ranchers for livestock killed by wolves. Rangers and other groups are also working to educate the public about the important role wolves play in ecosystems and to combat the big, bad wolf **stereotype**, which is based on misinformation. The hope is that knowledge increases the respect people have for wolves and wolf conservation.

ESSENTIAL QUESTION

How did the disappearance of wolves in Yellowstone National Park affect its ecosystem?

Remember how the disappearance of gray wolves affected beavers? In the next chapter, we'll look at this keystone species!

WHAT'S
YOUR OPINION?

IDEAS FOR SUPPLIES
- science journal
- pen, paper

The debate over the reintroduction of wolves is a heated one. Ranchers, hunters, pet owners, and conservationists have different opinions. Some people hate and fear wolves. Others love and respect them. Still others respect wolves but do not think they should be reintroduced. What do your family and friends think of the issue?

❯ **Generate survey questions, starting with "Do you think wolves should be introduced in the United States?"** Come up with three to five ways people might answer the question, such as "Yes," "No," "Needs more research." Create a chart listing your questions and possible answers.

❯ **Survey 10 or more friends, family members, teachers, or neighbors one at a time.** Ask the first respondent the first question and read them the possible answers. Circle the answer they choose. Repeat with other respondents.

❯ **Once you've completed your survey, create a bar graph or a pie chart for each question.** This will allow you to visually show the respondents' answers.

❯ **Analyze your results.** What is the opinion of your friends and family? Did you see any trends? Are there changes you would make to your survey questions or answers if you were going to run the survey again?

Try This

Go beyond the opinions and consider solutions. Perhaps the answer to wolf reintroduction isn't just yes or no but some kind of compromise. What would that compromise be? How could a compromise benefit all sides? If your state or region is one considering wolf reintroduction, you may want to send your survey results to your local officials.

TEXT TO WORLD

Do you have or know a dog? Have you spent time with dogs? What behaviors are similar to wolves?

SMELL THAT?

Wolves play an important role in their ecosystems because they are top predators. Their hunting helps keep the population of other animals in check, which has consequences throughout the ecosystem. When tracking prey, they rely on their incredible sense of smell, which is about 100 times better than ours. So how do humans use their sense of smell today?

You will need a partner for this activity.

> Each person collects five items and hides the items from the other person a distance away.

> Blindfold one person. The other brings one mystery item at a time toward the blindfolded person. The person carrying the mystery item should stop every few feet to ask the blindfolded person if they can smell the item.

> When the blindfolded person makes a guess about what the item is, record how far away the other person was. If the guess was correct, move on to the next item. If not, the partner with the mystery item should continue to move closer and the blindfolded person should continue to use their sense of smell to guess what the item is. Record whether the blindfolded person was able to identify each item and how far away the item was when it was identified.

> Switch places and repeat the experiment so each of you gets a chance to be blindfolded and to present mystery items to the other.

> What did you learn about your own sense of smell? Was the experiment easier or harder than you thought it would be? Which items were easiest to identify? Which were the hardest? Record your findings and thoughts in your journal.

> You might also consider trying this experiment outdoors on a day with a slight breeze. How does the wind affect what you can smell and how far away?

Try This

Take some time to think about all the ways we rely on our sense of smell, even in the modern world. We use it around food, to sense fire and other dangers, and more. Make a list of all the ways we use smell and rank them in order of importance. What would our lives be like if we had a reduced sense of smell or none at all?

Chapter 3

BRILLIANT
BEAVERS

To do their job as keystone species, predators must hunt and eat. But another type of keystone species has a different job. Ecosystem engineers are keystone species that modify entire ecosystems. Sometimes, they even create new ones.

The work they do provides or maintains vital habitats for other species and promotes biodiversity. Other species depend on them.

ESSENTIAL QUESTION

How do beavers transform ecosystems?

Beavers are ecosystem engineers. Beavers live in Europe and Asia as well as across North America. They inhabit woodlands and freshwater **riparian** environments, such as rivers, ponds, and marshes.

WORDS TO KNOW

riparian: related to the land at the edge of a stream, river, wetland, or other natural water source.

KEYSTONE SPECIES

WORDS TO KNOW

rodent: a mammal that uses its ever-growing front teeth to chew on things. Rodents make up more than half of all mammals on Earth and include mice, rats, squirrels, chipmunks, beavers, and gerbils.

amphibian: a cold-blooded animal, such as a toad, frog, or salamander, that needs sunlight to keep warm and shade to stay cool. Amphibians live on land and in the water.

vegetation: all the plant life in a particular area.

engineer: someone who designs or builds structures.

architect: someone who designs and oversees the construction of buildings.

TRANSFORMING THE LANDSCAPE

How does this **rodent** change entire ecosystems? Beavers start near a stream and cut down trees with their remarkable teeth and powerful jaws. The enamel on beavers' teeth is reinforced with iron, which makes their teeth extremely strong and reddish in color.

The beavers use the trees for both food and the construction of dams and lodges. Isn't cutting down trees a bad thing? Not always! When beavers cut down trees, they cut only what they need. Cutting down a few trees reduces the forest canopy so sunlight can reach the ground, which allows other plants and trees to grow.

Beavers are the second largest rodent in the world! The capybara of South America is the largest.

A beaver building a dam

After a tree falls, beavers cut it into smaller pieces. Then, they drag the branches through the water to build a dam across the stream. However, beavers don't live in the dams but in lodges. So, why do beavers go to all that trouble to build dams? To flood an area! A dam blocks a stream and results in a shallow pond where the beavers can then build their lodge. Having their lodge in the water keeps them safe from predators. The door to the lodge is underwater, and animals that hunt beavers, such as coyotes, bears, and foxes, aren't likely to risk a deep dive for food.

Check out this infographic for an introduction to beavers. How are beavers well-adapted to life in the water?

⌕ PBS beavers info

The largest beaver dam ever discovered is about a half mile long!

Dam construction has benefits that extend far beyond the beavers themselves. The most obvious result of a dam is a shallow, freshwater wetland that holds water. The new wetland becomes a habitat for many species, including other mammals, fish, turtles, **amphibians**, insects, water birds, and songbirds. It also increases **vegetation** along the wetland's edges.

Super Builders

In addition to being great **engineers** and plumbers, beavers are also excellent **architects**. Once they've created a pond, they build their lodge out of logs, sticks, stones, and mud. The mud plugs all the holes to keep frigid winter air out! Beavers do leave a vent at the top of the lodge to let fresh air in and gases out.

The only way into the lodge is through an underwater tunnel. Most lodges have two submerged entrances. Beavers line the floor of the lodge with grasses and vegetation. The end result is a warm, safe fortress with walls 2 to 3 feet thick. They tend to be 5 to 6 feet high and 12 feet wide.

Watch this PBS video to learn how beavers builder a dam. How do they build strong dams?

⌕ PBS beavers build dams video

WORDS TO KNOW

hydrology: the distribution and movement of water through an ecosystem.

evaporate: when a liquid heats up and changes into a gas, or vapor.

groundwater: water that is stored underground in soil, sand, and rocks.

aerate: to allow air to flow through.

drought: a long period of little or no rain.

watershed: an area of land that drains into a river or lake.

CALL THE PLUMBER

Not only are beavers engineers, but they are also plumbers! Their work changes the flow of water through an area. The change in **hydrology** alters the entire ecosystem.

Beaver dams slow a river's moving water and cause the water to spread out, creating a pond. The pond stores water, so it doesn't all run downstream or **evaporate**, giving the water time to seep into the ground, where it replenishes the **groundwater**.

Beaver ponds also regulate the flow of water downstream below the dam. This helps to keep water flowing all year round, which supports both plants and animals through dry seasons. Dams can help prevent downstream flooding and erosion during heavy rains or snowmelt.

Species Spotlight: Termites

Have you ever seen a termite? They're tiny! Believe it or not, termites are a keystone species and ecosystem engineer in Australian and African savannas.

Mound-building termites build enormous termite mounds. These mounds can be as tall as 16 feet! They also extend underground. The building of mounds improves the health of the soil. Not only does it cycle nutrients, it **aerates** the soil and allows water to soak into the ground more easily and stay moist for longer. All of this promotes plant growth. Large mounds offer protection for plants, while other species make use of the mounds for shelter, as lookout spots, or as a food source, feeding on the plants or termites.

In addition, the plumbing that beavers do cleans the water. All wetlands act as natural filters. Pollutants that run off from farms and urban areas are harmful to plants, wildlife, and humans. But, as contaminated water passes through wetlands, both sediment and pollutants are trapped. This filtering benefits the ecosystem and improves the quality of drinking water for humans.

In places where beaver ponds freeze over in the winter, beavers store branches for food at the bottom of the pond. The cold water acts like a refrigerator and beavers have food throughout the winter.

There's more: Like wolves and sharks, beavers are climate heroes! They reduce the effects of climate change. How? To start, the wetlands that beavers create store carbon. Remember, carbon dioxide is one of the greenhouses gases that causes the planet to warm when there's too much of it in the atmosphere.

The wetlands also offer protection from wildfires. Beaver ponds store water even in times of **drought**. The stored water provides moisture to the roots of plants and trees in the area and keeps vegetation from drying out and becoming fuel for a wildfire. Instead, the green and wet habitats help slow and even stop fires. This is especially important because the risk of wildfires increases as temperatures on Earth increase.

THREATS TO BEAVERS

Beavers are part of the food web wherever they live. That means they are prey for animals such as wolves and coyotes. But, not surprisingly, the main threat to beavers is people.

Before Europeans arrived in North America, beavers thrived in almost every stream, lake, and **watershed** across the continent. Scientists believe there were more than 60 million beavers at the time. Some estimates suggest there were more than 200 million! The work of those beavers shaped the land for millions of years.

KEYSTONE SPECIES

But when new settlers came to the continent, they did not see ecosystem engineers. They saw opportunity. The fur of beavers is thick and water resistant. Thus began the fur trade in North America.

Beavers were hunted and trapped in huge numbers. **Pelts** were used for fashionable men's hats and a chemical produced by beavers called **castoreum** was used for perfumes. People hunted beavers from coast to coast until the mid-1800s. Beavers in Europe and Asia suffered a similar fate.

But, just as fashion changes today, people's interest in such hats and perfumes faded. Hat makers turned to silk and fur prices dropped. The fur trade ended, but not before the beavers were almost extinct.

Luckily, beavers are resilient creatures. Once unregulated hunting ended, their numbers slowly rebounded. But the threat to beavers wasn't over. If you remember, beavers cause flooding and cut down trees. For these reasons, many people still consider them unwanted pests. Farmers are not especially happy to find their **crops** flooded by a beaver family that's moved in nearby.

A beaver dam in Denali National Park in Alaska

Sometimes, people remove and relocate the beavers. Other times, they kill them. And, as people develop more and more land for their own uses, beavers experience significant habitat loss.

Beaver ponds are considered Earth's kidneys because, like the body's kidneys, the ponds remove toxins from the environment.

CONSERVATION EFFORTS

At the time of the fur trade, people didn't realize how much beavers had shaped the land and how ecosystems suffered without them. People have since learned that beavers aren't making a mess of things but are making ecosystems healthier and increasing biodiversity. As a result, many states have laws regulating the destruction of beaver dams or the harming of beavers.

Still, beavers can be a nuisance. They flood fields, roads, and property and cut down trees people want to keep. Sometimes, beavers are a threat to human health. Beavers can carry a parasite called giardia, which can cause problems by infecting wells or being consumed by campers drinking from natural sources.

Scientist Spotlight: Emily Fairfax

After a devastating wildfire in California, scientist Emily Fairfax made an extraordinary discovery. Although the hillsides were charred and barren, the valley remained untouched by fire. Created by beavers, not only was this wet, green oasis unaffected, but it also served as a refuge for wildlife fleeing the fire. Further research revealed that riparian areas with beavers were three times less affected by wildfires than areas without beavers.

Fairfax's focus is **ecohydrology**. She studies riparian areas with beaver dams to better understand how beavers affect an area across time. Through her research, she's learned the value of the ecosystem services provided by beavers. She believes that we should see beavers as our partners in combating climate change.

KEYSTONE SPECIES

We need to balance the instincts and needs of beavers and the interests of their human neighbors. Science-based solutions can help people co-exist with beavers. Fences and tree trunk guards can keep beavers from cutting down trees on homeowners' property. Flow devices can reduce flooding by allowing some water to flow through, which keeps the beaver pond at a constant level.

Beavers also like to build dams in **culverts** under roads, which can cause dangerous flooding. Special fencing can keep beavers from doing this. Newer culverts are designed to prevent beavers from plugging them up.

> **One of the first beaver conservation efforts involved airplanes and parachutes.** Watch this video from 1948 to see for yourself. What do you think are the pros and cons of this plan for relocating beavers?
>
> 🔎 parachuting beavers video
>
> **PS**

The most hands-on conservation efforts are purposeful reintroductions of beavers into areas to restore ecosystems. In some cases, people even build a starter dam for the beavers. They hope that the starter dam deepens the stream enough that beavers feel safe and stay. In Washington State, beavers causing problems in urban areas were trapped and relocated to help restore salmon habitat and salmon populations. When the beavers returned, ponds and vegetation returned. This provided young salmon with critical shelter from predators and a food source.

> **ESSENTIAL QUESTION**
>
> How do beavers transform ecosystems?

Scientists continue to study how beavers restore ecosystems. The more we know, the more we can appreciate them and their work as ecosystem engineers.

In the next chapter, we'll learn about another keystone species that is also a bit misunderstood and underappreciated—alligators!

TEXT TO WORLD

What other creatures make their homes with entrances that are hard to access?

BUILD A
BEAVER DAM

Building a dam is a lot of work for a beaver. Build a model to understand the engineering, plumbing, and architecture that go into a beaver dam.

IDEAS FOR SUPPLIES

- a tub or tray at least 2 inches deep
- sticks, rocks, pinecones, and other plant material
- mud or clay
- water

❯ **Using your supplies, build a dam across the center of a tub or tray.** Make sure the dam goes all the way across and up the sides. Make it big and sturdy enough to hold water in one half of the tub or tray. Use rocks and mud or clay to fill in holes.

❯ **Once construction is complete, pour water on one side of the dam.** Beaver dams are not completely watertight but pay attention to how much and how fast water moves from one side to the "downstream" side.

❯ **How well did your dam hold up?** Would a beaver be satisfied with the dam? Which materials worked best? What other materials might you use to build a dam? What would you do differently next time?

Try This

Use your dam-building skills to make a model of a beaver lodge!

A DAY IN THE LIFE OF A
BUSY BEAVER

The phrase "busy as a beaver" came about because beavers spend lots of time building and maintaining their dams and lodges. They also spend time cutting down trees for food and building materials.

> To understand how busy beavers are, do some research about their habits and behavior. Take notes about how they spend their time.

> Think like a beaver! Create a journal entry as if you were one. Using a first-person point of view, describe how you spend your day. Write about all the building and eating you do and maybe other wildlife you encounter. Are there challenges during the day? Successes? Don't forget to include information about other members of your colony.

> Consider doing a journal entry for a different time of year. How does a beaver's life vary between seasons? In winter, many beaver ponds are frozen over. In spring and summer, there are beaver babies, called kits. What kinds of different foods are available? What wildlife is around at that time of year?

Try This

Make a comic book out of your beaver day! Create more characters and storylines and then draw everything in comic book format.

Chapter 4

ALL ABOUT
ALLIGATORS

Like sharks and wolves, American alligators are apex predators. Their dining habits contribute to the management of the populations of their prey. But it's their work as ecosystem engineers that makes them a keystone species.

American alligators are cold-blooded **reptiles**. They live in freshwater habitats in the American South, especially in Florida, Louisiana, and Alabama. They inhabit swamps, marshes, lakes, rivers, and other small bodies of water.

ESSENTIAL QUESTION

How is the work of alligators important to their ecosystems?

Since alligators are an apex predator, you probably guessed that they are carnivores—and they are not picky eaters. Alligators have powerful jaws that can crack open a turtle's shell. They'll also eat birds, fish, snakes, frogs, and mammals.

Alligators swallow most of their prey whole. With larger prey, alligators sometimes shake their heads side to side to break it into smaller pieces. Alligators also sometimes drag larger prey underwater to drown it.

HOW ALLIGATORS CHANGE ECOSYSTEMS

Alligators and their ancestors have been around for millions of years and even survived the mass extinction event that killed the dinosaurs.

One of the clearest examples of how alligators change ecosystems is in the Everglades in Florida. The Everglades is a **subtropical** wetland ecosystem that spans more than 1 million acres. It is not a swamp as many people think. Instead, nine different habitats—including mangrove forests and sawgrass marshes—are within this ecosystem. The entire region is sometimes called the "River of Grass" because of the shallow, slow-moving water that rises and falls with the seasons and travels more than 100 miles. In some places, it's 50 miles wide. For an alligator, it's the perfect habitat.

To understand the keystone role of alligators, you also need to understand the climate of their ecosystem. Alligators live in warm areas without cold winters but with a wet and dry season. The wet season is during the hot and humid summer months, when the Everglades gets almost 60 inches of rain!

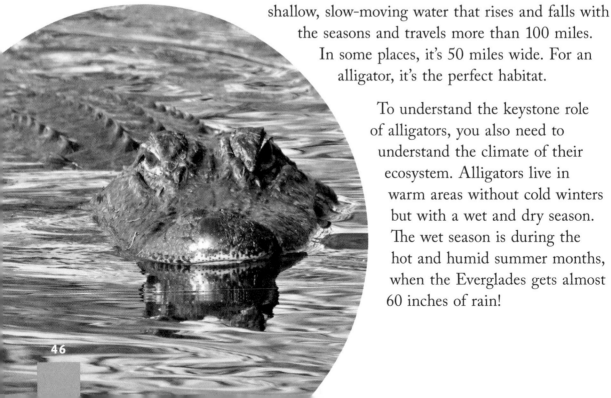

The dry season is during the winter months, when temperatures are mild but little rain falls.

Alligators do their best work before the dry season. They use their rounded snouts and claws to dig up vegetation to clear out channels. Then, they thrash their body and tail to create **wallows** that work like bathtubs and hold water throughout the

Check out this page created by the Everglades Foundation for interesting facts about alligators. Why is it important to learn about and understand alligators?

⌕ Everglades amazing alligators

dry season. Guess what these bathtubs are called? **Gator holes**! Across many years, an alligator may return to the same hole, making it larger each time. The work alligators do to create channels and wallows alters the landscape and affects the way water flows through it. As beavers do, alligators improve the hydrology of the ecosystem.

Species Spotlight: Peccaries

What does a cold-blooded reptile have in common with a pig-like ungulate? They are both ecosystem engineers and keystone species!

By regularly trampling and digging in the soil, peccaries create depressions that hold water much like alligators do. And, just like gator holes, these wallows often hold water through the dry season. They also provide important habitat for other species. Plus, peccaries forage in large numbers, which creates clearings. The clearings let in more light, allowing new plants to take root. By managing plant populations, peccaries help promote biodiversity. And after peccaries eat and digest, they've got to poop—when they do, seeds come out in their scat, spreading seeds throughout the forest.

KEYSTONE SPECIES

Gator holes are an important source of water during the dry season. They are even more valuable during droughts. Many species, in addition to alligators, use the holes. Birds, insects, fish, turtles, and other animals spend time in or near gator holes in the dry season.

Not only do these animals then have water, but they also have a place to find prey. Without this watery **refuge**, many animals would not survive the dry season.

Take a tour of the Everglades! Follow the Water will introduce you to the Everglades ecosystem, its history, and the species that live there. How is this ecosystem important to our planet?

🔎 Follow the Water

Why would other animals want to hang out with alligators for the whole dry season? Wouldn't they become part of an alligator buffet? Other predators also take refuge in these holes. But in the dry season, the risk of running out of water is greater than the risk of becoming dinner. It's a risk animals must take to survive.

A gator hole in the Everglades

Credit: Photo 220293421 © Francisco Blanco | Dreamstime.com

48

One reason alligators don't sit around eating everything in sight is that during the hot, dry months, they **aestivate**. That's the alligator equivalent to mammals **hibernating** during cold winter months. During aestivation, alligators' bodies slow down. They become inactive and conserve energy to survive the harsh conditions.

The Everglades has many species of plants and animals that are found nowhere else on Earth.

THREATS

Alligators, especially **juveniles**, do have a few natural predators. Raccoons, birds, and bobcats all prey on alligators. But like other keystone species you've already met, alligators' greatest threat comes from humans. In fact, hunting and habitat loss almost drove American alligators to extinction in the mid-1900s.

When European settlers arrived in the Everglades and surrounding regions, they did not see a thriving ecosystem. Instead, they thought it was a barren, useless swamp. They considered draining the wetlands to make it useful for their needs. By the 1880s, developers had turned that dream into a reality.

KEYSTONE SPECIES

WORDS TO KNOW

fragmented: broken down into smaller parts that are no longer connected to one another.

urbanization: the process of becoming more like a city.

invasive species: a nonnative plant or animal species that enters an ecosystem and spreads quickly, harming the system's balance.

breed: to produce offspring.

To make use of the land, settlers dug canals that drained the water out of the wetlands. But what is a wetland without water? The ecosystem began to collapse. The alligators and other species lost their habitat.

With the water gone, the land was used for agriculture, roads, homes, and businesses. Even more people moved to Florida during the early 1900s. The population soared, which increased the demand for more houses and roads. Developers dug even more canals. More of the Everglades was drained. Not only did wetlands disappear, but the hydrology of the whole ecosystem also changed. Instead of an intact river of grass, the Everglades was **fragmented** and developed, and the natural systems were destroyed. Such development reduced the area known as the River of Grass by 50 percent. Similar **urbanization** and human development occurred in alligator habitats across the American South.

Alligators' teeth are replaced throughout their lives when old ones fall out or are worn down. One alligator may have 3,000 teeth during its lifetime!

Visit this National Geographic page to learn more about the history and importance of the Endangered Species Act. How does the Endangered Species Act protect both animals and their habitats?

🔎 NatGeo endangered species act

In addition to destroying alligators' habitats, people ruthlessly hunted them. Like wolves and sharks, they were hated and feared, so they were killed. People also hunted alligators for their skin and meat. When the use of alligator hides in fashion became popular during the 1800s, people hunted alligators even more. Hunting became even simpler when boats and cars could get into alligator habitats. For hunters, it was an easy way to make good money.

An aerial view of the Everglades

Invasive species are a more recent threat to alligators. Burmese pythons showed up in the Everglades ecosystem in the late 1970s. No one knows for sure how they ended up in the Everglades, but probably pet snakes either escaped or were released. Since then, the snakes have been **breeding** and adapting. They can grow to more than 20 feet long, have no natural predators in the Everglades—and they prey on alligators. They also compete with alligators for habitat and food.

CONSERVATION EFFORTS

One turning point for alligators was during the first half of the 1900s. The settlers who drained alligators' ecosystems did not understand how ecosystems worked and saw the Everglades as a useless swamp. But as agricultural and urban development continued, a few people began to understand what was happening and voiced their concern.

One of those people was Ernest F. Coe (1866–1951), a landscape architect. In 1928, he started a campaign to have a national park established in the Everglades region because he was concerned about the species that lived there. Finally, in 1934, legislation was approved to create the Everglades National Park. In 1947, the park was officially established.

Another turning point for alligators was federal protection. In 1967, alligators were put on the very first list of endangered species in the United States. Later, alligators were listed under the Endangered Species Act of 1973, which gave them protection and called for preservation of their habitat.

The sex of a baby alligator is determined by the temperature of the egg in the nest. Cooler temperatures produce females and warmer temperatures produce males.

Scientist Spotlight: Marjory Stoneman Douglas

Marjory Stoneman Douglas (1890–1998) gave the Everglades its nickname, the River of Grass, and was on the front lines of the battle to save the Everglades.

During the early 1900s, Douglas wrote about conservation, as well as civil rights and women's rights, for a Miami, Florida, newspaper. In 1947, she published *The Everglades: River of Grass*. The book raised public interest in protecting the Everglades ecosystem.

In 1969, Douglas founded the Friends of the Everglades. Its initial project was to stop the construction of a large airport in the region. The group was successful! Douglas continued her conservationism throughout her lifetime. In 1993, she was awarded the Presidential Medal of Freedom by President Bill Clinton.

Marjorie Stoneman Douglas passed away in 1998 at the age of 108, but the work of Friends of the Everglades continues her conservation efforts. Learn more about what it does on its website.

🔎 Friends Everglades

Although these actions helped and alligator populations slowly increased, people were still illegally **poaching** alligators in Florida during the 1970s. Laws were strengthened to protect alligators, and their populations recovered enough that in 1987, they were removed from the Endangered Species list.

Still, decades of drainage and development had severely impacted the Everglades ecosystem. During the late 1900s, scientists, urban planners, and law makers began to develop a plan—a big one.

The plan was to restore the Everglades ecosystem. At the same time, people worked to address the need for water for a growing population and for protection against floods.

To learn more about the different habitats and plant communities within the Everglades, visit this National Park Service website. How are these ecosystems constantly changing?

🔎 NPS Everglades habitats

The Comprehensive Everglades Restoration Program (CERP) was approved by Congress in late 2000. The CERP involves both federal and state governments working together on dozens of projects to restore and protect much of alligators' habitat. That, combined with legal protection, ensures that this keystone species will be able to thrive in the American southeast.

So far, we've looked at creatures that walk on land and swim in water—what about critters that fly? In the next chapter, we'll learn all about bees!

ESSENTIAL QUESTION

How is the work of alligators important to their ecosystem?

VISIT

A WETLAND

The wetland ecosystems that beavers and alligators create and maintain provide habitat and slow, store, and filter water. They are found all over the world, and include tidal marshes, swamps, bogs, lagoons, and more. No matter their location or size, they support biodiversity. Time for a field trip!

❯ **Research wetlands near where you live.** Plan a visit that includes time to wander, explore, and sit.

❯ **During you visit, wander slowly and record the different species you see.** Include plants, animals, and insects. Look up in trees, on the ground, and in the water. Take photos or draw sketches of what you find.

❯ **Identify as many as you can by name.** Many parks provide species checklists that can help you identify the species you see.

❯ **Find a comfortable place to sit for 15 minutes or more.** Sit quietly without talking or moving. Just listen.

❯ **Describe the sounds around you.** Try to identify the additional species you hear.

❯ **What happened when you were quiet?** How did that change your observations?

❯ **Take a minute to brainstorm other species that you may not be able to see.**

Try This

At home, research the role of the different species in the wetland habitat you visited. Consider what would happen if one of these species disappeared. What would happen if the wetland were drained?

INTERVIEW AN
ALLIGATOR

IDEAS FOR
SUPPLIES
• science journal

One reason people hate and fear alligators is because they don't understand them. What better way to get to know them than through a personal interview?

> **If you could sit down and talk to an alligator, what questions would you ask?** Write down 5 to 10 questions. Use books or the internet to find the answers to your questions.

> **Compile the questions and answers in an interview format.** Do a written or podcast-style interview. In either case, think like an alligator.

* What would an alligator have to say?

* What is important to an alligator? Have the answers in the first person, as if the alligator is speaking.

Watch this video, *Dreaming of the Everglades,* **on the National Park Service website that traces the natural and human history of the Everglades.** What is the heartbeat of the Everglades? Why is it called that?

🔎 NPS Dreaming Everglades

Try This

The experiences of alligators have clearly changed throughout time. Do some time travel. Perhaps interview an alligator around the time of the dinosaurs or interview an alligator experiencing the draining and development of its habitat in the early 1900s. You could even travel to the future and imagine how alligators are surviving. No matter where you go in time, create interview questions, do the research, and create either a written or oral presentation.

TEXT TO **WORLD**

Do you feel scared to
meet an alligator?

GATOR HOLE
INFOGRAPHIC

IDEAS FOR SUPPLIES
- science journal
- posterboard
- art supplies

Alligators and their gator holes are vital to the ecosystems in which alligators live.

> **Find information about how alligators create their holes.** How wide and deep are they usually?

> **Research the other animals that rely on alligator holes during the dry season.** How many species need those gator holes?

> **Create a poster that shows the diversity of species in and around an alligator hole.** Label each species and include a sentence or two about it.

Try This

An alligator hole is its own ecosystem in the dry season. Within the hole are predators and prey. Using the information you collected, create a food web of the alligator hole ecosystem.

Wanna Wallow?

Alligators aren't the only animals that create or use wallows. The wallows create depressions in the ground that hold water and create a habitat and a water source for other species. Bison and peccaries both create wallows, too. The footsteps of elephants in soft soil creates wallows.

For other species, wallows are an important place to take a bath—a mud bath! The mud bath helps animals cool off and remove pests. Some animals even coat themselves in mud to create protection from the sun. Elephants, pigs, rhinos, deer, tapirs, warthogs, and Cape Buffalo like to wallow in mud.

Chapter 5

THE BUZZ ABOUT
BEES

Picture a bee. What type of bee do you see? More than 20,000 different species of bees exist in the world! In the United States, there are about 4,000 different species. These include honeybees, bumblebees, carpenter bees, and many more.

Bee species vary in size. The largest bee in the world is the appropriately named Wallace's giant bee. Females of this species are larger than males. They can grow to be 1.5 inches long. On the other hand, Perdita minima is the world's smallest bee. It is less than 0.08 inches long.

Bees are found on every continent on Earth except Antarctica. They thrive in a variety of habitats—forests, deserts, mountains, grasslands, and wetlands. They even live in the tundra of Alaska! Honeybees live in hives, but other bee species live in trees, underground, or in holes.

ESSENTIAL QUESTION

How do bees support biodiversity around the world?

KEYSTONE SPECIES

When you think of bees, what do you think of? Honey? Being stung? Some people are afraid of bees. But we should think of bees as vital pollinators wherever they live. Plants depend on them for pollination and bees depend on plants for food. Because of this relationship, bees are considered keystone mutualists.

Bees dance! Honeybees perform round dances and waggle dances to communicate to other bees where they can find good nectar nearby.

Mutualists are organisms with a relationship to another species that benefits both species. What affects one of the organisms also affects the other. Some mutualists are keystone species. In the case of bees, the entire ecosystem is impacted if the mutualistic relationship changes in any way.

A honeybee collecting nectar and helping with pollination

ROLE OF BEES

It might be hard to imagine that a tiny bee has such an enormous role on our planet. But, together, trillions of bees have a huge impact.

Most flowering plants need bees and other pollinators for **reproduction**. If plants can't reproduce, no more plants. **Pollination** requires **pollen** grains to be moved from the male part of one flower to the female parts of another.

If you've ever seen a honeycomb, you probably noticed that it is made of hundreds of connected hexagons. Watch this TedEd video to learn why the hexagon is the most effective architectural choice for honeybees. Why are bees considered good mathematicians?

🔎 TedEd honeybees hexagons

Species Spotlight: Green-backed Firecrown

Some species offer their ecosystem services to small areas. One of those is a hummingbird called a green-backed firecrown. These birds live in Patagonia, South America. Like bees, they are important keystone mutualists and pollinators.

The green-backed firecrowns feed on the nectar of flowering plants, shrubs, and trees where they live. In return, the hummingbirds move pollen from one plant to another. In fact, the hummingbird is responsible for pollinating 20 percent of the plants in the region. There are no other species there that can do this for the plants.

KEYSTONE SPECIES

WORDS TO KNOW

forage: to search for food.

fertilize: to join female and male cells to produce seeds and offspring.

sonication: the act of using sound to create vibrations to disrupt or shake something.

pesticide: a chemical used to kill pests such as rodents or insects.

That's where bees and other pollinators come in. Bees eat the nectar of flowering plants and trees. As they **forage**, pollen grains from the plant attach to them. Have you ever seen a bee that looks like it's covered in yellow dust? That's the pollen! When the bee goes to the next plant of the same type, some of the pollen falls off. This transfer of pollen from one plant to another **fertilizes** the plant so new seeds can develop.

The pollination performed by bees is important to all life on Earth. In one day, a single colony of bees can pollinate 300 million flowers. Pollination is needed for fruits, berries, nuts, and seeds to form and is vital to maintaining biodiversity. Healthy trees and plants also provide food sources for other animals. Plus, plants and trees provide habitats for animals. If bee populations decline, the entire ecosystem is affected.

In some flowers, the pollen may be hard to get to. On these flowers, some bees buzz. The vibration from the buzzing shakes the pollen loose so it lands on the bee. This process is called sonication, or buzz pollination.

AS LONG AS WE GIVE THEM SPACE WE SHOULD BE FINE AND THEY CAN DO THEIR JOB.

I'VE HEARD A BEE COLONY CAN POLLINATE MILLIONS OF FLOWERS IN A SINGLE DAY!

I CAN SEE WHY THEY ARE SO IMPORTANT TO LIFE ON EARTH!

Wild animals aren't the only ones that rely on bees for their food.

When you have your next meal, look at it before you eat. What ingredients in your meal needed pollinators to grow? On average, one in three bites of food that we eat is the result of pollination. Not only that, but 75 percent of all crops rely on pollination. Next time you have a snack, thank a bee!

THREATS

Despite the importance of bees, this keystone mutualist is in trouble because of human activity.

Pesticides are one of the biggest threats to bees. Farmers use pesticides to protect their crops from weeds and pests. Unfortunately, bees are also harmed and sometimes even killed. The chemicals in pesticides can affect the bees' nervous systems so they can't work as efficiently as they usually do.

They move more slowly, and they might get confused and fail to find their hive. Bees that do make it home often carry pesticides with them, which affects the whole colony.

Check out this website to see what goes on inside a honeybee hive and the roles different bees have. How are worker bees important to the health of the hive?

Whole Kids Inside Hive

KEYSTONE SPECIES

WORDS TO KNOW

monoculture farming: growing only a single type of crop at a time in a certain field.

malnourished: not receiving adequate amounts of food or nutrients.

varroa mites: tiny parasites that attach themselves to bees and spread disease though a colony.

colony collapse disorder (CCD): the disappearance of most of a colony's worker bees, leaving the queen and young bees, despite an ample supply of food.

citizen scientist: a volunteer who makes observations and collects scientific data to support the work of scientists.

Another threat is that bees' natural habitats are being destroyed. Even mowing a yard can destroy nesting sites for bees. Bees are also losing food sources. It's important for bees to eat a balanced diet, but that's often difficult in a world of **monoculture farming**. With only one type of crop, bees become **malnourished**. Poor nutrition leads to poor health.

Bees are also losing habitat because of climate change. Earth's rising temperatures affect where plants can grow—some die off and move north over time, altering bees' food supplies. Severe weather also disrupts habitats. Plus, the bees themselves cannot tolerate rising temperatures.

Other threats to bees include pollution, invasive species, pests, and disease. Studies have shown that pollution in the air affects bees' ability to smell flowers. When this happens, bees can't find food as easily as they normally do. And when they can't find food, they cannot pollinate as much. Bees' food sources are also affected by invasive species of plants. New plants often compete with native plants. Sometimes they push out native species. For bees, this means that the plants they rely on for food disappear.

Pests such as **varroa mites** affect bee populations as well. Varroa mites feed on honeybees in a colony. At the same time, these mites also pass on diseases that can spread through the colony.

Many bees become victims of **colony collapse disorder (CCD)**—the worker bees from a colony disappear but the queen and the young remain in the hive. Even with plenty of honey and pollen for the remaining bees, the colony collapses without the workers.

Several bee species are listed on the United States' Endangered Species List. When a species gets listed, scientists develop action plans to protect the species and its habitats.

The winter of 2006 to 2007—when 30 to 90 percent of hives in the United States were lost—was especially bad for domesticated bees. Normal losses are around 20 to 30 percent. Scientists are still working to find the cause of CCD. Possible factors include pests, disease, and pesticides.

CONSERVATION EFFORTS

One of the simplest, yet most effective bee conservation efforts is education. When people understand the importance of bees and the threats they face, they can be part of the solution. That includes you!

We can stop using harmful pesticides and herbicides. Convince your family to make your outdoor spaces safe for bees by going chemical-free. Or plant native plants, flowers, and trees that attract bees and other pollinators. Not only will you be providing food for the bees, but also habitat. You can have fun helping bees by creating a bee bath or a bee hotel. The baths provide water for thirsty bees and hotels give them a safe place to nest and rest.

> The Bee Conservancy has a list of 10 things that we can do to help save bees. Why do you think it's important to play a role in bee conservation?
>
> 🔎 Bee Conservancy 10

Citizens Scientists

The more we know about bees, the more effective our conservation efforts can be. And **citizen scientists** can add to that knowledge. Just as trillions of bees all over the world have a big impact, so do millions of people who work toward a common goal.

For bee conservation, everyday people collaborate with scientists. They contribute to bee research by collecting data about bee behaviors and bee populations. They help answer real-life questions. They contribute to new solutions to protect bees. Citizen scientists also work to educate others about the value of bees and how everyone can protect them.

> Learn more about becoming a citizen scientist to contribute to bee conservation. How could you help?
>
> 🔎 Citizen science bees

Farmers can also play an important role in bee conservation. They can reduce or eliminate the use of harmful chemicals. Farmers can switch from monoculture farming to planting different crops that promote biodiversity and support bees. They can also avoid mowing in certain seasons to avoid destroying nests.

World Bee Day is May 20! Visit this United Nations website to learn the many ways that people celebrate bees each year. How could you celebrate World Bee Day?

🔍 UN World Bee Day

In addition, farmers can plant trees, shrubs, and grasses in and around their fields. Wildflowers in and around fields are beneficial to bees. Another way farmers can support bees is by leaving some fields wild.

ESSENTIAL QUESTION

How do bees support biodiversity around the world?

All these simple steps increase biodiversity, food sources for bees, and bee habitat. The farmer benefits, too! Diverse plants attract pollinators to their crops. And some of the plants protect crops from wind and erosion.

To better protect bees, we need laws that prioritize their health and safety. In Europe, several harmful pesticides are already banned. In the United States, as of 2023, both the federal government and individual states were working to ban the sale of these pesticides.

Together, we can all play a role in protecting pollinators, including the flying foxes you'll meet in the next chapter!

TEXT TO **WORLD**

Do you like honey? Which of your foods might have to be replaced if we didn't have bees?

THANK
A POLLINATOR

Pollinators include not only bees, but also flies, butterflies, beetles, hummingbirds, bats (which we'll talk more about in the next chapter!), and more. They pollinate flowers, including crops, and are responsible for one in every three bites of food we eat. Investigate the role of pollinators in your next meal!

❯ **During your next meal, record what you eat in your science journal.** Be very detailed about what you write down. A sandwich isn't just a sandwich. It includes bread and possibly meats, cheeses, vegetables, and condiments.

❯ **After your meal, investigate every part of it.** Look at ingredients labels. What are the ingredients in bread? Mayonnaise? Cheese? Create a list of all the ingredients in your meal.

❯ **Research each ingredient on your list.** Did it come from a crop that required pollination? Record what you find.

❯ **Count the total number of ingredients on your list.** How many were from a crop that required pollination?

❯ **Create a poster or other visual to present your findings.** Include every part of your meal and every ingredient.

Bees aren't the world's only pollinators. Birds, bats, butterflies, moths, ants, flies, and other insects also pollinate plants. Even the wind helps to move pollen from one plant to another.

Try This

Repeat the research for different meals during the day. Were some more reliant on pollinators? Try surveying meals with recipes from different parts of the world. Are there noticeable differences between the number of ingredients that rely on pollinators in these meals? Try comparing a meal of just fresh, whole ingredients with a pre-packed boxed or frozen meal.

OPEN A
BEE RESTAURANT

Helping bees is as simple as opening a restaurant. Plant a pollinator garden at your home! You don't need a big yard or lots of space—you can grow flowers in pots, garden beds, window boxes, and more. Get creative!

❯ **Research the types of bees and native plants near you.** Use online resource or talk to local experts such as gardeners, people who work at a nursery, or park rangers.

❯ **Once you discover what your bee neighbors like to eat, identify native plants that grow at different times during the season—spring, summer, and into the fall.** Your bees will then have a reliable food source throughout the growing season!

❯ **Draw a plan to show where you'll place your seeds or plants.** Plan for the amount of sunlight and water each plant needs as well as how much heat it can tolerate.

❯ **Time to plant!** Follow the directions that came with your plants or seed packets. After you finish planting, make sure to water everything regularly.

IDEAS FOR SUPPLIES

- information about native local plants and pollinators
- soil
- trowel
- seeds
- water

A hotel for bees!

Try This

Bees aren't the only pollinators. Consider including plants in your garden that will attract a variety of pollinators, such as birds and butterflies. Once your plants begin to flower, note which pollinators visit which flowers. What time of day do they visit? Do visitors to your garden change throughout the season? Create a pollinator garden logbook to track what you observe.

DISSECT A
FLOWER

To better understand pollination and how flowers reproduce, crawl into a flower yourself!

IDEAS FOR SUPPLIES

- one large flower from a garden or florist (note: never take a flower out of someone's garden without permission)
- scissors or a knife
- tweezers

❯ **Once you have a flower head, carefully cut it open.** Then pull it open with the tweezers.

❯ **Using the diagram shown here, try to identify all the main parts of your flower:**

* petals
* anther
* filament
* sepal
* pollen grains
* stigma
* style
* ovary
* stem

petal
anther
stigma
pollen grains
style
filament
sepal
ovary
stem

❯ **Take photos or make a drawing of your dissected flower.** Label the parts.

Try This

Different flowers have different shapes, yet they all have the same parts. Collect different types of flowers and dissect them as well. Again, identify the parts. Create a visual to compare and contrast the flowers.

Chapter 6

FANTASTIC
FLYING FOXES

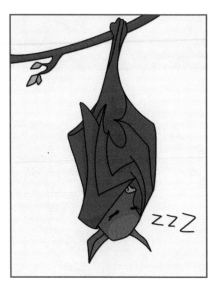

Flying foxes are not foxes at all. They're bats! There are dozens of species of flying foxes, living in subtropical and **tropical** climates on islands in the Indian Ocean and South Pacific. They are all **frugivorous**. In addition to fruit, they eat pollen and nectar. They use their excellent sense of sight and smell to find food. Their eyesight is so good that flying foxes can navigate in the dark.

ESSENTIAL QUESTION

What would happen if a keystone mutualist such as the flying fox disappeared from its ecosystem?

Flying foxes are keystone mutualists. They depend on the **flora** in their ecosystem for the fruit, pollen, and nectar they eat, and those plants depend on flying foxes for reproduction

ROLES OF THE FLYING FOX

Flying foxes play a key role in **seed dispersal** in the ecosystems where they live. Plants, trees, and flowers can't move themselves or their seeds, but they get help from the flying fox to scatter their seeds widely.

How do the bats do this? The bats eat fruit and flowers and then fly to another location. They digest their food and then they defecate, or poop. The seeds—which are unharmed—are deposited in a new location, where they can grow into new plants.

Bats are Earth's only flying mammal.

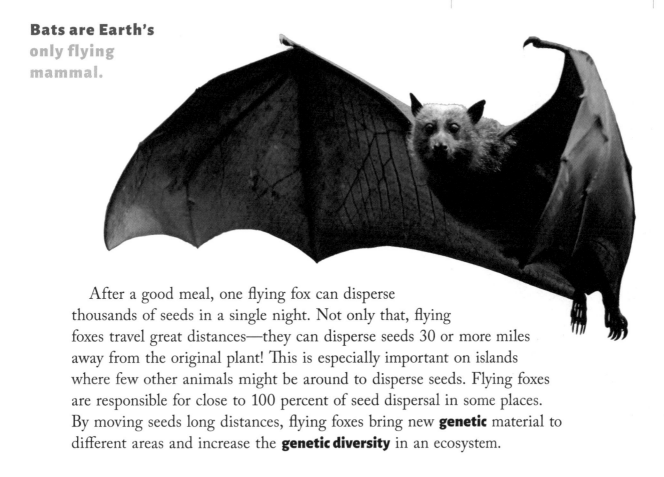

After a good meal, one flying fox can disperse thousands of seeds in a single night. Not only that, flying foxes travel great distances—they can disperse seeds 30 or more miles away from the original plant! This is especially important on islands where few other animals might be around to disperse seeds. Flying foxes are responsible for close to 100 percent of seed dispersal in some places. By moving seeds long distances, flying foxes bring new **genetic** material to different areas and increase the **genetic diversity** in an ecosystem.

KEYSTONE SPECIES

co-evolve: for one species to change slowly at the same time as another species in a way that benefits both species.

raptor: a bird of prey, such as an eagle, hawk, falcon, or owl, that hunts other animals.

High genetic diversity helps keep an ecosystem strong, healthy, and adaptable as well as more resilient in times of stress. An ecosystem with low genetic diversity is less adaptable and more likely to collapse. For individual species, low genetic diversity puts them at risk of extinction.

Flying foxes are also important pollinators in their ecosystems. When they move from plant to plant, they carry pollen from one to the other. And because of their large size, these bats can move a lot of pollen!

The bone structure of a bat's wing is like the bone structure of a human hand. The wings even have thumbs and wrists!

Flying foxes and the trees in their ecosystems have **co-evolved** for more than 40 million years. To start, the flowers on these trees only release pollen at night, which is when the flying foxes forage. The bats themselves have soft, furry bellies that pick up the pollen. Once the flying foxes arrive at the next flower, some of the pollen on their bellies falls off and fertilizes the flowers on that plant. As they do during seed dispersal, flying foxes carry pollen long distances.

Flying foxes dine on the flowers, nectar, and fruit of more than 300 species of plants.

THREATS

Flying foxes do have natural predators, including pythons, some species of **raptors**, and even crocodiles. But can you guess what their greatest threat is? Yes, humans. Habitat loss, the loss of native foods, and outright hunting have resulted in half of all flying fox species being at risk for extinction.

Flying foxes prefer roosting sites that are near water, have tall vegetation, and offer some protection from extreme temperatures.

In the video, wildlife ecologist Tim Pearson describes the natural history of bats and how conflicts with people affect flying foxes. In what ways are flying foxes and humans similar? Why is understanding these similarities important?

🔍 Sydney bats Tim Pearson

Species Spotlight: Agoutis

Agoutis live in the rainforests of Central and South America. In the Amazon, these medium-sized rodents are a keystone species thanks to their super-strong, sharp teeth. Other animals cannot break open the seed pod of Brazil nuts. But agoutis can! They use those super-strong, sharp teeth to break open the pods. This releases the seeds, the parts we call Brazil nuts. Agoutis then eat some of the 10 to 25 seeds and bury the rest to save for later. Those buried seeds are sometimes forgotten—they sprout and grow into new trees! Without agoutis, Brazil nut trees cannot reproduce. Over time, the loss of agoutis in the Amazon rainforest would mean the loss of Brazil nut trees, which would impact the entire ecosystem.

Credit: Hans Norelius (CC BY 2.0)

KEYSTONE SPECIES

Once it establishes a camp, a colony of flying foxes uses the site for decades. Some of today's camps in Australia have been occupied since the late 1800s! Unfortunately, many of these camps are under threat or have already been destroyed for development or agriculture.

Flying foxes are both intelligent and social. They feed alone, but at sunrise return to "camps" that can have hundreds of thousands of bats.

When native forests are cut down, flying foxes lose not only their habitat but also much of their food supply. The bats are forced to look somewhere else. Oftentimes, this is a **cultivated** orchard. Unfortunately, farmers aren't too happy about sharing their crops with a colony of bats. To get rid of the bats, farmers shoot, poison, or electrocute them—sometimes entire flying fox camps are burned to the ground.

The loss of native food sources often means flying foxes have to travel much farther to eat. Sometimes, these trips are too long, especially for young bats. The bats try to feed locally, but in some cases there is not enough food for a full colony, and many bats starve. Droughts have even more severe effects on the bats.

Flying foxes also fall victim to other human-made hazards such as pesticide and lead poisoning. Some bats get tangled in fruit tree netting. Flying foxes can collide with planes, cars, barbed wire, and electrical wires.

Unfortunately, centuries of misinformation and misunderstanding have given all bats a bad reputation. Movies and the media often portray bats as evil bloodsuckers to be feared and hated.

Check out this site for links to activity sheets and fun poems about bats. Why do you think it's important to keep learning about bats?

🔎 Sydney bats 4 kids

Blind as Bat

Have you ever heard the phrase, "blind as a bat"? As it turns out, that's an insult to bats! Small bats, sometimes called microbats, use **echolocation** to get around and find food. But they are not blind. Flying foxes, which are megabats, do not even have the ability to use echolocation. Instead they use their eyesight and sense of smell to locate food.

While in some ways, flying foxes don't see as well as people, they see better than us in other ways. Here's how it works. Animals, including us, have both rods and cones in their eyes. The rods are cells that help to see in dim light and to see objects that are moving quickly. Cones are what help to see details and to differentiate between colors. There are three types of cones. They allow us to see green, blue, and red wavelengths of light. Humans have all three types of cones, but most mammals—including flying foxes—only have two.

Flying foxes have the cones that allow them see blue and green light wavelengths, but not the red. So to a flying fox, everything appears blue or yellow. These bats also have fewer cones than people do. As a result, they do not see as many colors as we do and they do not see them as vividly. However, they have more rods! That means they have far better night vision than we do. And nighttime is when they do their foraging, which is not only good for them but also for the larger ecosystem.

KEYSTONE SPECIES

Part of our distrust of bats is rooted in the myth that bats carry all kinds of diseases that are a threat to humans. But the thing to remember is that people also carry diseases. As do dogs and cats. When it comes to flying foxes and other bats, the potential threat of the diseases they do carry is greatly exaggerated. Bats are very clean animals. They spend most of their lives high in trees or in caves away from people.

Human deaths associated with bats are rare. Most importantly, if people leave bats alone, bats leave people alone.

As for many other species, flying foxes are affected by climate change. As Earth warms, extreme heat and drought are more common. Flying foxes cannot tolerate the extreme heat, and droughts affect their food supply.

Flying foxes aren't the only species of bat in Australasia, the area that includes Australia, New Zealand, and some nearby Pacific islands. Visit the Australasian Bat Society's website to discover more of that region's amazing bats. What are some of the similarities and differences between the different bats in the region?

🔎 Ausbats our bats

Scientist Spotlight: Lawrence Pope

In Australia, Lawrence Pope (1961–) has made a name for himself in bat conservation. One of his big projects was to move grey-headed flying foxes out of Melbourne's Royal Botanic Gardens. During the 1980s, the bats had moved in due to habitat loss, but were killing and damaging many rare trees in the gardens.

To keep the bats from being shot, during the early 2000s, Pope began a campaign of noise harassment at dawn and dusk to scare the bats away. The bats scattered across the city and after a few months finally regrouped in Yarra Bend Park, a large natural park in the Melbourne area. There, they roost in peace.

CONSERVATION EFFORTS

Since bats are so misunderstood and unappreciated, education is one of the keys to bat conservation. We need to educate individuals, governments, and wildlife workers about the benefits of bats. People can learn that bats are not scary but helpful! If we understand and respect bats, we can help protect them.

Flying foxes are extremely social. They like to hang out with friends and family. They even have a complex system of communication, which is what makes flying fox camps so noisy!

As more people understand the truth about bats, they can work to pass laws to protect these mammals. Many species of flying fox are listed as endangered in the countries where they live, which helps protect them. In Australia, for example, the grey-headed flying fox was put on a list of threatened species in 2001, after a 30-percent decrease in population. The listing protects the bats from illegal killing. It also calls for identifying and protecting key habitats where the bats roost and forage. Further, the plan includes public education about the value of bats as well as how to coexist with them.

KEYSTONE SPECIES

Sanctuaries are another solution to protecting bats. In the Philippines, the Mabuwaya Foundation successfully fought for the preservation of a flying fox roosting site that was home to tens of thousands of bats. In 2015, the foundation established a 3,200-acre sanctuary and is using former hunters as guards at the sanctuary. This foundation also works to change people's minds about bats.

Other conservation groups work with local communities to protect bats. In Indonesia, the conservation group Progres Sulawesi worked with locals in the village of Salu and educated them about what bats do for the ecosystem. People helped count bats and planted trees and cleaned beaches to protect bat habitats. This kind of local involvement **empowers** the community and changes its perception of bats as well as reduces the hunting of bats. During four years of conservation, the population of flying foxes rose from 8,000 to 40,000!

To stop bats from roosting in urban trees or eating orchard fruit, people are using sound. They blare various electric noises near the trees people want to protect. The noises are stressful to the bats and encourage them to go somewhere else. Another method is to put python feces on the trees. Since pythons are one of flying foxes' main predators, the bats think the snakes are near and avoid the area.

As more people come to see that bats aren't to be feared but appreciated, conservation efforts to help them will likely become even more widespread.

In the next chapter, let's swoop back to the earth and learn about wildebeests!

Bat Con, based in the United States, works around the world to help bats. Visit the website to learn more about bats and the work that Bat Con does. Why do you think they call bats unlikely heroes?

🔍 batcon 101

ESSENTIAL QUESTION

What would happen if a keystone mutualist such as the flying fox disappeared from its ecosystem?

TEXT TO **WORLD**

Have you ever had a bat trapped in your house or apartment? What was your first reaction?

SEEING COLOR

The visible light that bats and all other animals (including us) see is energy released as light wavelengths. Within these wavelengths are a variety of colors. Red has the longest wavelength, while blue has the shortest. The primary colors of light are red, green, and blue. All other colors are some combination of those three!

This might sound a bit different from what you've heard when mixing paint or crayon colors. In those cases, the primary colors are red, blue, and yellow. Slightly confusing, yes. But, remember that the colors our eyes perceive are red, green, and blue, and how we see those colors depends on how an object absorbs or reflects the red, green, and blue light wavelengths. Think about a red fire truck. We perceive it as red because the truck absorbs the green and blue light and reflects the red.

To better understand this, a short experiment will reveal how different color light wavelengths are absorbed or reflected by surfaces of different colors.

❯ **Inside the white paper cup, color the bottom and sides into stripes of the three primary light colors: green, blue, and red.** Leave one stripe white, so you end up with four stripes – green, blue, red, and white.

❯ **Punch a hole in the bottom center of the cup with a pen.**

❯ **Plug in the holiday lights and find a red bulb.** Stick that bulb into the bottom of the cup. Turn off the lights in the room.

❯ **Look at the green, blue, and red stripes in the cup.** Do the colors inside the cup look the same? Did they change?

❯ **Try the experiment using the green and then blue light bulb.** How do the colors change depending on the color of the light bulb? Why does this happen?

Try This

Color another cup with a different set of colors, such as orange, yellow, purple, pink, and black. Try shining different colored lights in the cup. What do you see? How can you explain those colors?

ODE TO A
FLYING FOX

An ode is a type of lyric poem that celebrates or praises someone for all their wonderful traits. Lyric poems use emotions and express feelings, often speaking directly to the person (or thing) being praised. Flying foxes are not people, but we should celebrate and praise them, too!

> Use print or online resources as well as the information in this chapter to take notes about the importance of flying foxes.

> Do some research about how to write an ode. Look at example poems for kids.

> Write an ode to flying foxes. Your ode can rhyme, but it doesn't need to. It can be silly or serious. Use lots of adjectives. Exaggerate. Most importantly, get emotional!

Use this website to start your exploration of odes. It includes kid-friendly examples of odes.

🔎 Poetry4Kids ode

Try This

Think about other forms of poetry, including haiku, limericks, acrostics, and more. Write another type of poem about flying foxes. Create a small poster with one of your poems and a picture of a flying fox.

CREATE A
BROCHURE

IDEAS FOR SUPPLIES
- paper
- art supplies

As keystone mutualists, flying foxes are vital to maintaining healthy ecosystems. Yet, as you've read, the bats face many challenges. Create a descriptive brochure that educates others about the value of one species of flying fox.

❯ **Select one species of flying fox you'd like to learn more about.** Research your flying fox. Take notes on where it lives, the habitat it prefers, its appearance, and what it eats. Be sure to find information about the keystone role of your flying fox as well as the threats to it.

❯ **To make the brochure, lay a regular sheet of plain paper horizontally.** Then, fold it into thirds. You should have six panels (three on the front and three on the back). Close the brochure to determine which panel is your front cover. Find or draw an image of your flying fox on the cover and include a title for your brochure.

❯ **Organize your information and plan where to put it on the different panels.** Place the information on the panels. Use headings and subheadings for each section and add more pictures or images.

Try This

Since flying foxes are mutualists, do additional research about the seed dispersal and pollination your species of flying fox performs. If this bat disappeared, what effect would that have on the ecosystem? Which plants might disappear also? What other animals depend on those plants? Add this information to your brochure or create another brochure.

Chapter 7

WILD ABOUT
WILDEBEESTS

When you think of African wildlife, what comes to mind? Lions and giraffes? Zebras, elephants, and hippos? These are the animals that capture our attention. They are the stars of stories and movies. But what about wildebeests? They don't get nearly as much credit as they should!

Wildebeests live on the grassy plains of eastern and southern Africa. They are ungulates closely related to antelopes, but wildebeests are much stockier. They also have a mane and tail like horses. Both males and females sport beards and have horns. Wildebeests travel in herds of hundreds of animals to help protect themselves against predators.

ESSENTIAL QUESTION

Why are the huge numbers of wildebeests and their Great Migration vital to the ecosystem of the East African plains?

WORDS TO KNOW

Serengeti: a vast grassland and woodland plains ecosystem in east-central Africa. In the native Maasai language the name means "endless plains."

cull: to kill a select number of animals to control their numbers.

Scientists were surprised when they learned herbivores can be keystone species. All they do is eat plants! But researchers soon discovered that some herbivores act like nature's gardeners. They trim the grass and manage their ecosystem through their foraging. The work they do promotes biodiversity and strengthens the whole system.

ROLE OF WILDEBEEST

When Robert Paine made his first discoveries about keystone species, scientists were focused on top predators as keystone species. But around the same time, a man named Tony Sinclair (1944–) discovered that herbivores can be keystone species, too.

In the case of the wildebeests, their numbers declined greatly in the Serengeti during the early 1900s due to a virus. As the wildebeests rebounded during the 1960s, their numbers rose quickly. Scientists wondered if the large number of wildebeests would overgraze the grasslands and destroy habitats for other animals. Some wanted the animals **culled** to avoid an ecosystem collapse. Tony Sinclair and other scientists convinced park officials to wait to see what would happen.

Because of their gardening services, wildebeests are nicknamed "the lawnmowers of the **Serengeti**."

Learn more about the life and characteristics of wildebeests on the African Wildlife Foundation website. Are there any wildebeest facts that surprise you?

AWF wildebeest

It turned out that the grasslands were transformed. In time, the number of wildebeests leveled off and stayed at 1.4 million animals. They reached their natural population balance.

KEYSTONE SPECIES

nomadic: always on the move.

mortality rate: the number of deaths.

Although the larger number of wildebeests ate more grass, less grass meant less fuel for wildfires in the dry season. With less burning and less intense fires, trees had a chance to sprout. Plus, since wildebeests do not eat trees, small trees could grow and provide food and habitat for giraffes, elephants, and many other species. With the return of all these animals, predators such as lions also came back. As biodiversity increased in the region, everything reconnected. The whole ecosystem was stronger than it had been without a large population of wildebeests.

Not only do the areas with wildebeests experience fewer wildfires, but they also store more carbon. And for that, wildebeests are considered climate heroes.

How do wildebeests manage the vast East African ecosystem? Wildebeests are **nomadic** and are on the move year-round. The migration they are part of includes more than 2 million animals such as zebras and other grazers.

The Great Migration is one of Earth's greatest natural wonders due to its enormous size and scale.

In what is called the "Great Migration," the animals follow an enormous clockwise loop in search of food. When the rainy season ends in one region, they move on to the next area where food and water are available. The migration loop covers more than 1,800 miles and spans both Tanzania and Kenya.

THREATS

On the East African plains, wildebeests do have natural predators. These include lions, cheetahs, leopards, crocodiles, and hyenas. Yet, as with all predator-prey relationships, the result is a balance in the ecosystem. Predators need to eat to maintain their populations. And their hunting helps to keep wildebeest populations in check. So, although the predators are a threat to young, weak, and old wildebeests, the population of wildebeests is not at risk if the ecosystem is in balance.

Watch wildebeest and other animals on the move in this video. Why is it important to study migration as climate change alters the availability of food and water?

Harry Collins wildebeest

However, during the late 1800s, wildebeests were exposed to a new threat—domestic cattle. The cattle themselves were not the problem, but the virus they passed on to wildebeests and other African ungulates was. The virus, sometimes known as "cattle plague," was highly contagious and spread through wildebeest herds like a cold spreads in a school from classroom to classroom. The **mortality rate** was very high.

Scientist Spotlight: Paula Kahumbu

Paula Kahumbu (1966–) grew up in Kenya, surrounded by wildlife. Based in Kenya, she is now one of Africa's leading wildlife conservationists. She studied ecology and evolutionary biology and eventually turned to conservation. She wanted to help the animals in Kenya by becoming a voice for them.

Kahumbu turned to storytelling. Through her stories and documentaries, she entertains and educates to inspire others to conserve and protect the land and its wildlife. Much of her work focuses on children, with the goal of inspiring a new generation of African conservationists.

KEYSTONE SPECIES

WORDS TO KNOW

snare: a trap to catch wildlife.

bushmeat: the meat of wild animals in Africa.

tourism: the business of people traveling for fun.

A vaccine for cattle was finally invented during the mid-1900s. Still, by the 1960s, the wildebeest population was at an all-time low. Instead of more than a million, only a few hundred thousand wildebeests remained.

Within minutes of being born, a wildebeest calf can stand and run. This adaptation helps them avoid predators.

The wildebeest population has since rebounded. But it still faces threats. One of the greatest is habitat fragmentation due to human development. Sometimes, people put up fences to protect agricultural areas. These impact the habitat, movements, and migration patterns of wildebeests.

Migrating wildebeests also get caught in wire **snares**. Poachers lay out webs of these wire snares to hunt **bushmeat**. The wildebeests do not see the wire as they move, and when they walk into it, the wire gets caught on their legs, heads, or horns. Snared animals that aren't eventually killed by the poachers die slowly due to wounds or because they cannot move.

Another threat to wildebeests is **tourism**. Many people travel to East Africa on safaris to see all the great wildlife. One of the favorite migration viewing spots for tourists is at the Mara River.

This PBS video reveals the dangers of the river crossing for wildebeests and other animals. How does mass crossing help the wildebeests? How does it help the crocodiles? Please note this video contains graphic scenes of predator-prey relationships.

🔎 PBS wildebeest crocodile

This is one of the most dramatic and dangerous parts of the migration route because the wildebeests must cross a river that is full of crocodiles. An increased number of tour vehicles put the herds in even greater danger. The vehicles scare and confuse the wildebeests. Sometimes, vehicles even block the migration route and stop the wildebeests from crossing the river. This forces the wildebeests to find a different route that is not familiar to them and is often more dangerous.

The Great Migration of wildebeests and other grazers is Earth's largest animal migration.

Credit: Matt Scobel (CC BY 3.0)

CONSERVATION EFFORTS

The first intervention that helped wildebeests was not a conservation effort. It was the vaccination to save cattle. The huge losses of domesticated cattle in Africa due to the cattle plague was devastating for humans. It led to widespread starvation and a loss of income.

So, the vaccine was important to people who kept cattle. But once cattle were vaccinated against the virus, wildebeests no longer got the virus, either. Their populations began to recover. Scientists watched the wildebeest numbers increase on the grassy plains. It was then that Tony Sinclair and other scientists witnessed the transformation of the ecosystem and discovered that wildebeests are a keystone species.

To address the effects of habitat fragmentation, scientists monitor wildebeests and collect data. They want to understand how fragmentation affects wildebeest behavior. To do this, they have fitted some wildebeests with collars that have **GPS** trackers. These trackers give scientists the information they need to understand how much space the herds require. It also helps them identify important migration **corridors**. This information can guide both community and government planning to support wildebeest conservation.

Species Spotlight: African Forest Elephant

Another keystone herbivore in Africa is the forest elephant. They are sometimes called "mega-gardeners," though their pruning techniques are not neat and tidy. These elephants trample on and eat young trees as they forage. Sometimes, they even knock down bigger trees. This creates open spaces where light can reach the forest floor so other species of plants can grow. This increases the biodiversity of both plants and animals in the forest.

Forest elephants eat a lot, too. And you know what that means! They poop a lot. But that's a good thing! Because dung is rich in nutrients, it fertilizes the soil. Plus, the dung piles become mini habitats. Insects, fungi, and even frogs live and thrive in elephant dung. All the pooping also disperses seeds throughout the forest.

To protect wildebeests from the snares laid by poachers at the border between Tanzania and Kenya, patrol teams go out every day when the Great Migration is coming through.

Some nights, poachers set out as many as 200 snares. During the day, several dozen rangers move through dense bushes trying to find and remove as many as they can. Not only do they collect snares, they also help the animals they find entangled in wire. Several rangers might have to work together to unwrap a wire from an animal's leg or horn. Tens of thousands of animals are poached yearly in the area. Rangers know that their work is vital to maintaining wildlife populations.

Some tourism practices do put wildebeests at risk, but tourism itself is important to the economy of the region. It can also help fund conservation efforts. The balance lies in **sustainable tourism**, which means following practices that keep animals safe and minimize the impact on the environment.

Plus, tourism protects and supports local communities. Tourism creates jobs and brings money into a region. Both visitors and local people can learn about the importance of biodiversity and how to change their behaviors to protect it. These effects extend far beyond one tour or one village. They become key factors for conservation worldwide.

In the next chapter, we'll meet another herbivore keystone creature— the bison!

ESSENTIAL QUESTION

Why are the huge numbers of wildebeests and their Great Migration vital to the ecosystem of the East African plains?

WILDEBEEST
MIGRATION

IDEAS FOR SUPPLIES
- research materials
- map of East Africa

Every year, more than 1 million wildebeests and other animals migrate across great distances in East Africa. Let's research the Great Migration and map it.

❯ **Collect background information about the Great Migration from books or online.**

❯ **Find a blank map of East Africa or draw one.** Use arrows to show the route the wildebeests take.

❯ **Add information about the time of year the wildebeests are in certain locations.** Include a title, map key, and compass rose. Label the different countries and regions the herds travel through.

Learn more about the Great Migration on Expert Africa's site, which includes moving migration maps and a video about the stages of the migration throughout a year. What might be the impact if the Great Migration was interrupted?

🔎 Expert Africa wildebeest

Try This

Add more information to your map. When is mating season for wildebeests? Where are they when the calves born? Consider including facts about the wet and dry seasons. Add details about the miles traveled to reveal the scale of the migration.

TEXT TO WORLD

Are there any animal migrations that happen where you live?

AFRICAN SAVANNA
FOOD WEB

IDEAS FOR SUPPLIES
- note cards
- pencils or pens for drawing
- string

Food webs reveal the complex, interconnected relationships among species in an ecosystem. Wildebeests are one part of the food web in the plains of East Africa.

> **Research information about the food web on the Serengeti or Masa Mari.** Be sure to collect information about predators, **consumers**, producers, and **decomposers**.

> **On one side of a note card, put the name of one species of plant or animal and draw its picture.** On the reverse side of the note card, add details about that species, including what it eats and what eats it.

> **Create at least 10 note cards.** Lay the note cards out on a flat surface and think about how the species on the cards are related to one another.

> **Use cut pieces of string to make the connections between species.** Then, create a more permanent display. You could put the note cards and string on posterboard, photograph them, or tape them to a wall (with permission!).

Try This

Add more species, including insects, to your food web. Can you reach 20 species in your web? How about 30? Consider other factors such as weather and fire that can affect your web. Now select one species. Consider what would happen if that one species disappeared.

WORDS TO KNOW

consumer: an organism that eats other organisms.

decomposer: an organism such as ants, fungi, and worms that break down waste, dead plants, and animals.

Chapter 8

BURLY
BISON

On the other side of the world from wildebeests lives another keystone herbivore—bison. These ungulates have massive shaggy heads, a hump over their shoulders, and horns. Bison live in large herds on the North American prairies. They graze there year-round. Their preferred meal is grass, but they sometimes eat flowers, the leaves of **woody plants**, and **lichen**.

ESSENTIAL QUESTION

Why is it important to restore the bison to the North American Great Plains?

For more than 10,000 years, bison herds have shaped the North American prairie ecosystem as well as Native American culture.

ROLE OF BISON

Bison have a pretty simple job. They don't need to hunt or pollinate. They don't have to build or dig anything. Their migrations are much shorter than that of wildebeests. All bison must do is eat and poop—and they do a lot of both, producing lots of **manure**!

The largest bison can weigh as much as a small car.

How does this vegetarian help the prairie? Like the wildebeests, the job of bison is to eat grass, especially in areas where wildfires have swept through. Bison prefer burned areas because in those areas, grasses are the first plants to grow back. The bison don't have to eat around other plants in search of grasses.

KEYSTONE SPECIES

WORDS TO KNOW

nutrient cycle: the way nutrients move through living and nonliving things in an ecosystem.

microorganism: an organism so small it can be seen only under a microscope.

Also, grass often takes over and pushes out other plants. Grazing bison result in less grass so other plants have a chance to grow. More light, water, and nutrients are available for new plants. All of this increases the diversity of plants in the ecosystem.

Bison's grazing habits also create a quilt-like pattern of plants. Since bison eat mostly grass, they graze in some areas and leave areas with plants other than grasses alone. The greater plant diversity and quilt-like growth pattern create new habitats for birds, insects, and other species.

One study revealed that native plant species increased by 86 percent in areas where bison grazed.

One of these species is the greater-prairie chicken, which relies on this quilt of various habitats. The chickens use different areas for different activities, such as nesting and mating. Other animals, such as prairie dogs, prefer grazed areas where it's easier to spot approaching predators.

Pronghorns rely on bison for snow removal in the winter. Pronghorns can't dig through snow themselves. But bison sweep their huge heads back and forth to remove snow and reach vegetation. In very deep snow, bison act like snowplows, creating pathways for pronghorns and other animals.

This fungus loves to grow on bison dung!

Bison help the ecosystem in other ways too. As they move across the prairie, seeds hitch a ride on their fur, so seeds are dispersed over great distances. Bison hooves aerate the soil as the animals walk, which lets more air and water into the ground, making it healthier. Further, the trampling pushes seeds into the ground and the hoof prints create depressions where water can collect.

Bison can hear and smell well but have poor vision. They can also run up to 35 miles per hour!

After all the bison eat, they do a lot of pooping. Each bison produces 10 to 12 quarts of dung a day. That's like filling a 2½- to 3-gallon-sized milk jug! Each deposit is full of nutrients important to the **nutrient cycle** in the prairie ecosystem. The dung not only fertilizes the soil, it also supports **microorganism** and insect communities. One bison patty may be home to nearly 300 different insect species! Of course, all these insects make great meals for other species, including birds, turtles, and bats.

Species Spotlight: Prairie Dogs

Bison often share their habitat with prairie dogs, which are another keystone species. These small rodents live in large colonies in underground burrow systems. All the digging they do is important to their ecosystem. It loosens the soil, which lets in more air and water so plant roots grow better and take in more nutrients. Like bison, prairie dogs also graze. This keeps woody plants from taking over and allows flowers to grow. The biodiversity of plants and animals is greater in areas where prairie dogs live.

Abandoned prairie dog burrows are also valuable real estate. Many other species use the burrows, including the endangered black-footed ferret. Burrowing owls, snakes, and foxes use the burrows, too. And one more thing—prairie dogs are part of the ecosystem food web. They are a food source for many predators, including hawks and other raptors, coyotes, badgers, and snakes.

KEYSTONE SPECIES

In addition to eating and pooping, bison create wallows when they roll around on the ground to shed their winter coat or to get rid of insects. The rolling creates a depression in the ground that holds water. The depression benefits both plant and animal species, especially during dry periods. For example, some amphibians use the wallows for breeding. Other animals use the wallows as a source of drinking water.

THREATS

No one knows exactly how many bison roamed the prairies of North America before 1800. Some estimates put the number at 30 million. Other estimates are closer to 100 million. No matter the total number, a lot of bison were on the continent!

Bison have a few natural predators, including grizzly bears and wolves. Yet, as with other keystone species you've met in this book, the greatest threat to bison is humans.

Throughout history, bison dung has also been important to people. In places without wood to burn for heat and cooking, people would dry and burn bison patties.

When Native Americans hunted bison, they took only what they needed so bison populations stayed steady. Settlers, though, killed bison by the millions throughout the 1800s. A lot of the killing was backed by the United States government. At the time, settlers were at war with Native peoples over land. The United States knew how important bison were to the culture and values of the Plains Indians. By getting rid of bison, the government hoped it could gain control of Native peoples and their land.

The completion of the **Transcontinental Railroad** in 1869 contributed to the destruction of both Native tribes and bison. The railroad allowed troops and supplies to move around quickly and easily.

Across the West, the army destroyed Native American villages, food supplies, livestock, and shelter. And the railroad made hunting much easier. Settlers traveled widely and killed countless numbers of bison. The enormous losses of bison put Native Americans at risk because they no longer had a way to feed and support themselves.

In other cases, bison hunting was done simply for sport. Sometimes, people killed bison to make money. Photographs from the time reveal mountainous piles of bison skulls showing off the dominance of man over nature. This slaughter of bison almost led to their extinction.

Watch these bison live cams to see bison out on the plains roaming and foraging. In the spring, you might even get a glimpse of new calves! If there aren't any bison in the area, check back another day. Why do you think having these live cams available to the public is important?

🔍 Explore bison livecam

By the end of the 1800s, fewer than 1,000 bison remained. Only two small wild herds were left. One lived in Yellowstone National Park and the other was in Canada in northern Alberta. A few captive bison lived in zoos or on privately owned ranches.

Native Americans and Bison

Bison play an important role in the culture of Native Americans in North America.

For thousands of years, they hunted bison for food and used their **hides** for clothing and shelter. They crafted tools and weapons from bison bones. Nothing went to waste. Bison were essential to the survival of Native peoples.

Yet, to Native Americans then and now, bison are more than that. They are spirit animals. Native Americans are grateful to the bison for their gift of life and celebrate them in prayers, dances, and songs. In recent years, drawing from the connections they have shared with these special animals, Native Nations have been heavily involved in restoring bison to the grasslands of the Plains.

KEYSTONE SPECIES

WORDS TO KNOW

taxidermist: a person who prepares, stuffs, and mounts the skins of animals to look lifelike.

Another threat to bison was—and still is—habitat loss. As settlers moved across North America, they cleared land for farming and ranching. They put up fences and established towns, roads, and homes. This human activity, combined with the loss of bison, destroyed much of the prairie ecosystem. Less than half of the original U.S. grassland ecosystem remains.

People sometimes use the word "buffalo" for bison, but the two are not closely related. Perhaps when European settlers first saw bison in North America, they thought they were the Old World buffalo they were familiar with.

CONSERVATION EFFORTS

The conservation of bison began during the late 1800s. In 1874, the U.S. government outlawed the hunting of bison on federal land. Then, in 1886, a man named William Temple Hornaday (1854–1937) went to Montana to collect bison specimens for the National Museum.

He was a **taxidermist** who wanted to preserve animals for future generations to see. Hornaday was shocked to discover that the enormous herds of bison he'd seen on an earlier trip were gone.

A former hunter himself, Hornaday turned conservationist. Along with the specimens he collected to stuff and mount for the museum, Hornaday captured several live bison. This might not sound like a way to help bison, but Hornaday had a plan. He took the animals back to Washington, DC, where he put them on display. He hoped to capture people's attention and teach them about bison and what was happening to them. And he wanted people to be inspired to be part of environmental conservation.

Read this article to learn about the differences between bison and buffalo and how to tell them apart. What are some similarities and differences between bison and buffalo?

🔍 Treehugger bison buffalo

His plan worked. The bison were extremely popular. They brought much-needed attention to a species facing extinction. Hornaday is often credited with starting the conservation movement in the United States.

Secretary of Interior Deb Haaland

Secretary Deb Haaland (1960–) of the Pueblo of Laguna tribe is the first Native American to become a U.S. cabinet secretary, leading the Department of the Interior. This department oversees the protection and management of natural resources. It also honors cultural heritage. Her position and her work give voice to Native American concerns and a boost to bison conservation.

In 2023, $25 million was set aside for bison conservation. Haaland announced that Indigenous knowledge would be used as the guide to conservation. The effort calls for building new herds and continuing to return bison to Native tribal land. Native peoples will once again be the stewards of bison on Native lands.

KEYSTONE SPECIES

Beginning during the early 1900s, conservation of bison was the combined effort of conservationists, scientists, and lawmakers. In 1902, Yellowstone National Park purchased and raised 21 bison. As time passed, those bison mixed with bison from the remaining wild bison in the park. By the middle of the century, the population in Yellowstone was up to 1,300.

Visit the Smithsonian Institution archives to see photos of William Temple Hornaday's career and the bison he brought back to Washington. What challenges might Hornaday have faced bringing live bison from the West to Washington, DC?

🔍 SI Archives Hornaday

Other conservation efforts focused on breeding in captivity to promote genetic diversity. Wild reserves for bison were created in other parts of the country. The goal was not only to conserve bison but also to restore the prairie ecosystem.

Native Americans are playing a key role in returning bison to Native lands. The Intertribal Buffalo Council (ITBC) was established in 1992. Now, at least 80 tribes are managing more than 20,000 bison on tribal lands. Rosebud Sioux tribe member Troy Heinert stated, "Our goal and mission is to restore buffalo back to Indian country for that cultural and spiritual connection that Indigenous people have with the buffalo."

ESSENTIAL QUESTION

Why is it important to restore the bison to the North American Great Plains?

Since efforts began during the early 1900s, bison have been reintroduced to several different areas across North America. Although the number of wild bison is on the rise, the species still depends on conservation management for survival. Still, the collective efforts of Native Tribes, ranchers, and conservationists have had a remarkable impact on bison populations. Their numbers went from only a few hundred wild bison during the late 1800s to more than 15,000 as of 2023.

Collective conservation efforts are also underway for another keystone species that is very different from the others we've discussed so far—coral!

TEXT TO **WORLD**

Why are people more likely to support conservation efforts for a species they have a personal connection to?

COMPARE AND
CONTRAST

Bison greatly affect the prairie ecosystem, so prairies where bison live and graze are very different from those without bison. Compare and contrast a prairie with and without bison.

❯ **Research the North American prairie and the plants and animals that live there.** What do bison do for the ecosystem? What happens when they are removed? Or, if they've been absent from a region, what happens when they return?

❯ **Use the information to create a Venn diagram.** How are prairies with bison different from those without bison? How are they the same? Use the diagram to create a poster that represents your findings.

National Bison Day is celebrated each year on the first Saturday of November.

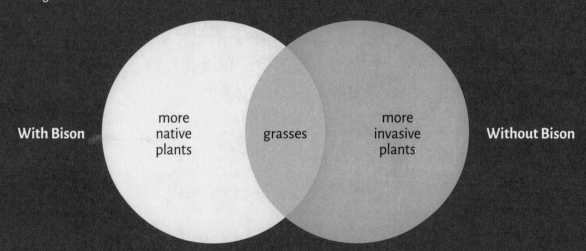

With Bison — more native plants — grasses — more invasive plants — Without Bison

Try This

Learn more about other species affected by bison. Consider not only mammals and birds but also reptiles, amphibians, insects, and plants. Add details to your Venn diagram and to your visual. Label the organisms and include a sentence or two about each.

SOIL AERATION

IDEAS FOR SUPPLIES
- two shallow pans
- soil
- quick-growing grass seeds
- straw
- water

Bison are important to soil health because their hooves aerate the soil as they walk, transport seeds, and push seeds into the soil. See for yourself how important this process is.

❯ **Each pan represents a grassland.** Fill both with about 1 inch of soil. Pat it down lightly.

❯ **Distribute seeds over one-half of each pan.** Try to use the same number of seeds in each. Do not push the seeds into the soil.

❯ **Water both pans evenly with the same amount of water in each.** Set one pan aside. That's your control pan.

❯ **Take your straw and poke it gently into the dirt of the second pan, simulating the footsteps of bison on the grasslands.** Be sure to take "footsteps" through the area you seeded and all over the pan. Place both pans in a sunny spot.

❯ **Make predictions.** How do you think the grass will grow in each pan? Will the growth be the same? Why or why not? Write your hypothesis in your science journal.

❯ **Monitor both pans, watering equally as needed.** The soil should be slightly damp, but not saturated.

❯ **Observe the pans each day and record what you see.** Are the grasses growing similarly in both pans?

Try This

Repeat the experiment to simulate different size footsteps in the soil (such as a chopstick or skewer, or the lid from a milk jug). You might also experiment with applying different amounts of pressure on the soil with different footsteps. Take notes as you go about the location of different footsteps in different pans. Record your findings and compare.

Chapter 9

CRAZY ABOUT
CORALS

ARE CORALS UNDERWATER PLANTS? OR ROCKS? I CAN'T TELL.

ACCORDING TO THIS, NEITHER. THEY'RE ACTUALLY LIVING CREATURES.

THEY LOOK SO ALIEN!

Coral reefs may look like rocks or plants—but they are neither! The coral polyps that make up a reef are tiny invertebrates. The polyps themselves are soft like their closest cousins, sea anemones and jellyfish. But these reef-building corals build a hard exoskeleton made of calcium carbonate around their bodies.

Corals also have tiny, single-celled algae called **zooxanthellae** living inside them. That might sound gross, but it's a good thing! Those zooxanthellae produce oxygen for the corals. They also contain the **chlorophyll** that uses photosynthesis to turn the sun's energy into food for the coral polyps. In exchange, the zooxanthellae have a safe place to live protected by the corals' hard exoskeleton. Corals get their bright colors from these zooxanthellae.

ESSENTIAL QUESTION

Why are coral reefs sometimes called rainforests of the sea?

KEYSTONE SPECIES

Reef-building coral polyps are small. Most are less than one-half-inch wide, although some can grow to 5 inches. Corals live in large colonies, and many colonies together form a reef.

Reef formation takes a long, long time. It starts when coral **larvae** attach themselves to a rock or another hard surface underwater. There, they grow slowly, between a tenth of an inch to 4 inches per year. It can take a reef more than 10,000 years to form! The Great Barrier Reef off the coast of Australia is the world's largest reef. It is about 20,000 years old.

Find out more about corals and reef habitats, plus look at a video that puts viewers underwater at a reef! How many different marine species can you spot?

🔎 RMG what coral

Corals live in oceans around the world in both shallow and deep water. The corals that build reefs are usually found in tropical and subtropical waters that are less than 150 feet deep. These reef-building corals are a keystone species.

ROLE OF CORALS IN THE OCEAN

Are you wondering how hard, fixed-in-place corals are a keystone species? They don't move. They don't hunt, forage, or pollinate. But they do build!

Corals are a keystone species because the reefs they build are vital to life in the ocean. Even though reefs are found on less than 1 percent of the sea floor, more than one-quarter of all marine species rely on the reefs for survival. For this reason, coral are considered a foundational species—they create and maintain entire ecosystems. It is also why coral reefs are often called the "rainforests of the sea." On land, if trees in the rainforest disappear, the rainforest ecosystem goes away. The same is true in the ocean. Without corals, the reef ecosystem disappears.

You've probably seen pictures of tropical coral reefs surrounded by fish, sea turtles, seahorses, squid, crabs, starfish, octopuses, sponges, and many other marine species. The reefs provide a place for these species to find food. In the marine world, a reef is a giant buffet with something for everyone!

Reef-building corals are cousins to jellyfish and sea anemones.

Some species of fish eat corals despite their hard exoskeletons. They feed on soft coral tissue. Other fish feed on algae and other small organisms on the reef. Still other marine species are carnivorous—they visit coral reefs to find prey that live and feed there. For example, sharks and other predators can find smaller fish on the reef to dine on. And crabs and others scavenge the ocean floor around the reef for their food.

WORDS TO KNOW

spawn: to produce and deposit eggs.

cyclone: the name of a hurricane over the Indian Ocean, the Bay of Bengal, and Australia.

hurricane: a tropical storm with sustained winds of at least 74 miles per hour and a definite rotation around a central point.

Coral reefs provide shelter for many species, too. Those nooks and crannies are perfect places for smaller species to hide from predators. They are also places for species to **spawn** and to raise their young.

Because so many marine species rely on coral reefs, corals play a huge role in supporting biodiversity in the ocean. If corals die, the result is a trophic cascade as the ecosystem collapses.

THREATS

While coral reefs seem strong, they are quite fragile. Natural threats to corals include storms and disease. Huge waves caused by **cyclones** and **hurricanes** can break and damage coral reefs, scattering the pieces. Since corals grow so slowly, it can take reefs decades to recover from just one powerful storm.

This video by the Natural History Museum in London, England, explores the value of coral reefs to both wild species and humans. In what ways are coral reefs important to humans?

🔎 NHM why coral reefs

THAT CORAL HAS A FRIEND!

HEY, LITTLE CRAB!

I'VE HEARD CORAL REEFS ARE REALLY IMPORTANT BECAUSE THEY PROVIDE SHELTER AND FOOD FOR LOTS OF OTHER ANIMALS.

Sometimes, extended low tides leave corals out of the water longer than normal. When this happens, the corals can dry out or overheat. Natural predators are another threat to corals if their populations are not kept in check by predators higher up the food chain.

Some corals live 4,000 years or more! Scientists can tell how old they are because they have growth rings, just like trees do.

The greatest threat to corals, though, is climate change. One effect of climate change is more frequent and more intense storms. While some damage to coral reefs is normal, human-driven climate change is making storms worse. Stronger storms cause more damage to coral reefs.

Check out the infographics by the National Oceanic and Atmospheric Administration (NOAA). One reveals how coral reefs are affected by climate change. The other explains the land-based sources of ocean pollution. Why is it important to share this information with the world?

🔎 NOAA coral reef climate

An unhealthy coral reef

acidification: when there is too much carbon dioxide in the air or ocean, making it more acidic.

acidic: from acids, which are chemical compounds that taste sour, bitter, or tart. Examples are vinegar and lemon juice. Water also contains some acid.

coral bleaching: coral that turns white, indicating it is ill and dying.

Ocean **acidification** is another result of climate change. Oceans naturally absorb carbon dioxide from the air. But today, the levels of carbon dioxide in the atmosphere are so high and oceans are absorbing so much more carbon dioxide, they are becoming too **acidic**. This acidity makes it difficult for shelled organisms, including corals, to build and maintain their hard calcium carbonate skeletons. Reefs become more fragile. If oceans become too acidic, scientists predict that the reefs may even begin to dissolve.

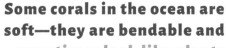

Some corals in the ocean are soft—they are bendable and sometimes look like plants or trees. Soft corals do not form coral reefs.

Global warming has caused ocean temperatures to rise, and warmer water puts stress on corals. How? Disease outbreaks among corals are increasing and more reef-building corals are dying.

Warmer water has also caused mass **coral bleaching**. When the water gets too warm, coral polyps force out the zooxanthellae. Without the food produced by the algae, the corals turn white. When this happens, the coral polyps don't die, but they are more fragile and vulnerable to damage and disease.

If all those threats aren't enough, fishing, water pollution, marine debris, and even sunscreen also affect coral reefs. Sometimes, people harvest corals to sell for aquariums or to make jewelry. Other times, too much fishing affects the number of fish on a reef. The entire reef ecosystem becomes unbalanced. Fishing techniques can also harm reefs. Boat anchors break and damage corals, as do nets dragged along the ocean floor.

Listen to this NOAA podcast to learn more about coral bleaching. What are the dangers of coral bleaching?

🔎 NOAA podcast bleaching

Pollution that affects coral reefs often starts on land. Sewage, chemicals, pesticides, sediment, and more all get washed into the ocean and can be toxic. The pollutants can affect corals' ability to reproduce and grow or can cause disease. In some cases, these pollutants increase nutrient levels in the water, which promotes algae growth. Too many algae can smother corals.

Marine debris can smother corals, as well as damage and break corals. Finally, some of the sunscreens that we wear when enjoying coral reefs have chemical ingredients that harm coral. As a result of all these threats, 50 percent of Earth's coral reefs were lost between 1950 and 2021.

Coral Farmer

Ken Nedimyer began diving in the Florida Keys as a kid. As decades passed, he saw the reefs die and the fish disappear. He decided to do something about this— through coral farming.

Nedimyer noticed that when staghorn coral larvae attached themselves to rocks in his aquaculture farm, coral started growing. With his daughter's help, Nedimyer cut pieces of the growing coral and attached it to other rocks. It worked! Nedimyer took pieces of coral to the dying reef and attached them there. That worked, too! With the help of a team of volunteers, Nedimyer has kept improving his coral farming techniques and has grown thousands of colonies of corals.

WORDS TO KNOW

renewable energy: a form of energy that doesn't get used up, including the energy of the sun and the wind.

CONSERVATION EFFORTS

The threats facing the ocean may seem overwhelming! But many conservation efforts are underway. Since climate change is one of the leading threats to coral reefs, cutting carbon emissions is key to coral reef conservation. Many countries and states have set goals to reduce carbon emissions and stop global warming. This includes reducing the use of fossil fuels and increasing the use of **renewable energy**.

The world's oceans contain approximately 6,000 different species of corals.

The creation of Marine Protected Areas (MPAs) is another way to help keep reefs healthy. MPAs are the ocean version of land-based national parks or wilderness areas. MPAs around the world offer different levels of protection. MPAs in the United States include the Florida Keys National Marine Sanctuary and the Papahānaumokuākea Marine National Monument in Hawaii as well as parts of the Great Lakes and areas off both coasts. In some MPAs, no fishing is allowed at all. Others allow limited fishing and other activities. Monitoring has shown that the most restricted MPAs have the best outcomes.

Have a look at the NOAA's infographic to learn about protecting coral reefs. What can you do?

NOAA coral infographic

Efforts are also taking place to actively restore coral reefs. Conservationists grow corals underwater by attaching small fragments of healthy corals to manmade, treelike structures in an ocean nursery. After the coral grows to a certain size, it's taken from the nursery and planted on a reef. The goal is for the corals to spawn and produce more corals.

Species Spotlight: Parrotfish

Thousands of species of fish rely on coral reefs at some point in their lives. One of those is the parrotfish. And while parrotfish depend on reefs, corals depend on parrotfish. They are a keystone species, too. Parrotfish spend their days grazing with their fused, beak-like front teeth. They scrape off and eat algae on the corals, keeping the reefs clean. Without the parrotfish, the algae can smother and kill the corals. The fish also chomp off dead coral, giving new corals a place to grow.

Credit: Rickard Zerpe (CC BY 2.0)

One last thing about parrotfish—when they eat stony corals, they digest the corals bits. It passes through their system and comes out the other end as sand!

Scientists are working to identify corals that are resistant to climate change. While rising ocean temperatures cause bleaching in many corals, some seem better able to handle the stress. These corals have adapted to warmer waters.

For scientists, this offers hope. Coral nurseries can focus conservation efforts on the species of corals that have adapted to help restore reefs that are damaged or diseased. When these corals reproduce, the resilient traits will spread through the reef, making the whole reef stronger.

In the United States, NOAA is responsible for reef conservation. Through its Coral Reef Conservation Program (CRCP), scientists monitor reefs in the United States, study the causes of coral reef decline, and brainstorm solutions. CRCP is also involved in coral research and restoration.

In this National Geographic video, watch researcher Paola Rodriguez explain the threats to coral reefs and the monitoring and restoring of reefs she's undertaking. How is her work key to conservation?

🔍 Nat Geo Paola Rodriguez

As we've learned, conservation efforts are built on science and teamwork. We can easily get discouraged when we think about the work we still have to do to save keystone species and their ecosystems, but we can also see this as an exciting opportunity. We are learning more and more about the natural world and how each species has its role. What role do you think humans are going to play in keeping the planet healthy?

ESSENTIAL QUESTION

Why are coral reefs sometimes called rainforests of the sea?

Coral Reefs Are Important to People

Coral reefs are important to the marine ecosystem—and to people. Reefs create habitats for thousands of species of fish. These reef fish are vital food sources for half a billion people around the world.

In addition, most reefs are in shallow waters near coastlines. During storms, reefs act as a buffer, slowing down the waves. They absorb more than 95 percent of the waves' energy. Reefs also protect coastlines from erosion and flooding.

Finally, coral reefs attract millions of tourists of year. Tourism provides jobs and brings money to coastal communities. In many places, local economies are largely dependent on tourism.

HOME
SWEET HOME

A healthy coral reef is home to dozens of species of coral and other marine species. To better understand these highly diverse ecosystems, create a visual of a coral reef.

> **Select a coral reef somewhere on Earth.** Research what kinds of coral live there and the species that depend on that reef. Take notes on at least 10 different species.

> **Decide how you want to share your information visually.** You could create a poster, collage, or even a 3-D model.

> **Label the different species in your project.** These labels should include the services each species provides to the reef system.

> **Create a food web of the species on the coral reef to add to your project.**

IDEAS FOR SUPPLIES

- science journal
- art supplies such as clay, construction paper, colored pencils, markers, glue, posterboard

Healthy reefs are busy places, full of sounds — snaps, chirps, clicks, songs, grunts, and more. Visit this website to listen to the sound recordings of a healthy reef and of a reef after coral bleaching. Scroll down the page to the four recordings. What surprised you about the sounds on a healthy reef? What is the difference between a healthy reef and one that's been bleached? What does sound tell scientists about the health of the reefs?

🔍 coral reef healthy noise

Try This

Different species rely on reef habitat for different reasons. Add information to your visual that explains how each species depends on the coral reef and the other species there. Add additional species to your visual to further reveal the complexity of coral reef ecosystems.

*TEXT TO **WORLD***

What can you do to help support keystone species where you live?

OCEAN
ACIDIFICATION

As carbon dioxide levels in our atmosphere rise, the ocean absorbs more of it. The result is that the ocean has become more acidic. This makes it more difficult for animals to make shells. It also affects how quickly coral polyps grow their external skeletons and how strong they are. This makes coral reefs more fragile and less likely to recover when damaged.

❯ **Place an egg in the jar.** Pour vinegar into the jar so it covers the egg. The vinegar is acidic. What do you think will happen to the egg? Write your hypothesis in your science journal. Leave the egg in the jar for at least two days.

Get a closer look at the effects of ocean acidification in the NOAA's video. How are the choices we make on land affecting the ocean?

🔎 NOAA acidification

❯ **When it's time to remove the egg, be careful!** Use a plate or shallow basin. What happened to the egg? Make note of how it feels and what it looks like. What would happen to a sea creature or a coral with a shell or skeleton like that?

Try This

Redo the experiment using seashells instead of an egg. Again make predictions. You might also want to have several different jars of vinegar diluted with different amounts of water. This would simulate different levels of acidity in the ocean. Take notes on how the seashells feel and what they look like every day for a week or longer.

IS YOUR
SUNSCREEN
ECO-FRIENDLY?

IDEAS FOR SUPPLIES
- posterboard
- markers

If you are going to be outdoors in the sun, you should wear sunscreen. It protects your skin from harmful sun rays. But not all sunscreens are created equal. Not only do they vary in how well they protect our skin, but they also vary in ingredients. Some of those ingredients can harm water quality, corals, and other species.

An estimated 14,000 tons of sunscreen enter the ocean every year. Not only that, 15 percent of coral reefs in the world are impacted by the ingredients in sunscreen. But there are things we can all do to help, including knowing what's in our sunscreen and spreading the word.

> **Research sunscreen ingredients to find out which are harmful to corals.** Which chemicals are the most harmful to corals? What other chemicals impact corals? Which chemicals are safest, biodegradable, and mineral-based? Make a list.

> **Find sunscreen bottles in your home and read the ingredient labels.** Do they include any harmful chemicals?

> **Go to a store or visit with friends to investigate the ingredient labels on different types of sunscreen.**

> **Organize your research.** Which brands of sunscreen contain the most harmful chemicals? Which contain only some harmful chemicals? Which are fully reef-friendly?

> **Create a poster that shows the types of sunscreens that are reef-friendly and those that are not.** Include what you learned about how some ingredients harm water quality and coral reefs. Add information to your poster about alternatives to wearing sunscreen, such as swim shirts and hats. Ask permission to display this at school or elsewhere in the community to help inform others.

Try This

Do an experiment to see how well different types of reef-friendly sunscreen work! Include your findings in your public awareness campaign.

GLOSSARY

acidic: from acids, which are chemical compounds that taste sour, bitter, or tart. Examples are vinegar and lemon juice. Water also contains some acid.

acidification: when there is too much carbon dioxide in the air or ocean, making it more acidic.

adaptable: able to change to new or different conditions.

aerate: to allow air to flow through.

aerial: relating to the air.

aestivate: to pass hot, dry months with reduced activity and slowed body functions such as heart rate, similar to how some animals hibernate in the winter.

algae: a plant-like organism that lives in water and grows by converting energy from the sun into food.

amphibian: a cold-blooded animal, such as a toad, frog, or salamander, that needs sunlight to keep warm and shade to stay cool. Amphibians live on land and in the water.

apex predator: a species at the top of the food chain with no natural predators of its own.

architect: someone who designs and oversees the construction of buildings.

arid: very dry, receiving little rain.

atmosphere: the layer of gases around the earth.

biodiversity: the variety of life on Earth.

breed: to produce offspring.

buoyancy: inclined to stay afloat.

bushmeat: the meat of wild animals in Africa.

bycatch: marine species caught accidentally in a net while fishing for other species.

calcium carbonate: a compound found in bones and shells that forms limestone, a sedimentary rock.

carbon cycle: the movement of carbon through ecosystems.

carbon dioxide (CO_2): a colorless, odorless gas. Humans and animals exhale this gas while plants absorb it. It is also a byproduct of burning fossil fuels.

carnivore: an animal that eats other animals.

carnivorous: describes a carnivore, a plant or animal that eats only animals.

cartilage: tough, fibrous connective tissue. Our ears and nose are made of cartilage.

castoreum: a substance collected from the glands of beavers.

chlorophyll: a substance that makes plants green. It is used in photosynthesis to capture light energy.

citizen scientist: a volunteer who makes observations and collects scientific data to support the work of scientists.

climate change: a change in long-term weather patterns, which can happen through natural or manmade processes.

co-evolve: for one species to change slowly at the same time as another species in a way that benefits both species.

colony collapse disorder (CCD): the disappearance of most of a colony's worker bees, leaving the queen and young bees, despite an ample supply of food.

conservation: managing and protecting natural resources.

conservationist: a person who works to preserve nature.

consumer: an organism that eats other organisms.

coral bleaching: coral that turns white, indicating it is ill and dying.

corridor: in environmental science, a passageway that connects habitats for wildlife.

crops: plants grown for food and other uses.

cull: to kill a select number of animals to control their numbers.

cultivate: to develop land to grow crops or trees.

culvert: a tunnel that carries water under roads or railroad tracks.

cyclone: the name of a hurricane over the Indian Ocean, the Bay of Bengal, and Australia.

data: facts and observations about something.

decomposer: an organism such as ants, fungi, and worms that break down waste, dead plants, and animals.

dense: how tightly the matter in an object is packed.

drought: a long period of little or no rain.

echolocation: the ability to sense surroundings using soundwaves.

ecohydrology: the study of the movement and presence of water in an ecosystem and how it interacts with both living and nonliving things in the ecosystem.

ecologist: a scientist who studies the interaction between organisms and their environment.

ecology: the study of the patterns of relationship between species in an ecosystem.

ecosystem: an interdependent community of living and nonliving things and their environment.

ecosystem engineer: a species that greatly alters an ecosystem by creating, modifying, maintaining, or destroying it.

empower: to give someone authority and power.

engineer: someone who designs or builds structures.

erosion: the gradual wearing away of sand, soil, or rock by water or wind.

evaporate: when a liquid heats up and changes into a gas, or vapor.

exoskeleton: a hard shell or cover on the outside of an organism that provides support and protection.

extinction: the death of an entire species so that it no longer exists.

GLOSSARY

fertilize: to join female and male cells to produce seeds and offspring.

filter feeder: an animal that gets its food by filtering food particles or tiny living things from water.

flora: plant life.

food chain: a community of plants and animals where each is eaten by another higher up on the chain.

food web: a network of connected food chains.

forage: to search for food.

fossil: the remains of any living thing, including animals and plants, that have been preserved in rock.

fossil fuel: a natural fuel that formed long ago from the remains of living organisms. Coal, oil, and natural gas are fossil fuels.

foundational species: a species that provides the base on which an entire ecosystem is built.

fragmented: broken down into smaller parts that are no longer connected to one another.

frugivorous: feeding on fruit.

gator hole: a bathtub-like hole that alligators create using their snout, tail, and claws. The hole fills with water and provides refuge throughout the dry season.

genetic: related to traits that are passed on from one generation of animals or plants to the next.

genetic diversity: different or similar traits between two individuals in a species.

global warming: an increase in the average temperature of the earth's atmosphere, enough to cause climate change.

GPS: stands for global positioning system and is a system of satellites, computers, and receivers that can determine the exact location of a receiver anywhere on the planet.

greenhouse gas: a gas in the atmosphere that traps heat. We need some greenhouse gases, but too many trap too much heat and contribute to global warming.

groundwater: water that is stored underground in soil, sand, and rocks.

habitat: a plant's or animal's home, which supplies it with food, water, and shelter.

herbivore: an animal that eats only plants.

hibernate: to go into a deep sleep for many months with a low body temperature and heart rate.

hide: the skin of an animal.

hurricane: a tropical storm with sustained winds of at least 74 miles per hour and a definite rotation around a central point.

hydrology: the distribution and movement of water through an ecosystem.

hyperkeystone species: a species that can have an ecological impact on the entire planet.

hypothesis: an unproven idea that tries to explain certain facts or observations.

ichthyology: the study of fish.

invasive species: a nonnative plant or animal species that enters an ecosystem and spreads quickly, harming the system's balance.

invertebrate: an animal without a backbone.

juvenile: a young animal.

keystone: a central stone at the top of an arch that locks the whole together. Also, the central part of a system.

keystone species: a species that plays an essential role in an ecosystem and without which the ecosystem would be greatly altered.

larva: an organism at the beginning stage of development. Plural is larvae.

lichen: a plant-like organism made of algae and fungus that grows on solid surfaces such as rocks or trees.

livestock: farm and ranch animals, such as cows, horses, and sheep, that are raised for food and other products.

malnourished: not receiving adequate amounts of food or nutrients.

mammal: a type of animal, such as a human, dog, or cat. Mammals are born live, feed milk to their young, and usually have hair or fur covering most of their skin.

manure: solid waste.

marine: having to do with the ocean.

mate: to reproduce.

microorganism: an organism so small it can be seen only under a microscope.

migrate: to move from one environment to another when seasons change.

monoculture farming: growing only a single type of crop at a time in a certain field.

mortality rate: the number of deaths.

mutualists: two or more species in an ecosystem that interact in such a way that both benefit.

nomadic: always on the move.

nutrient cycle: the way nutrients move through living and nonliving things in an ecosystem.

nutrients: substances in food, water, and soil that living things need to live and grow.

organism: any living thing, such as a plant or animal.

pelt: an animal skin.

pesticide: a chemical used to kill pests such as rodents or insects.

PhD: doctor of philosophy, the highest degree in an area of study given by a college or university.

photosynthesis: the process a plant goes through to make its food. The plant uses water and carbon dioxide in the presence of sunlight to make oxygen and sugar.

plankton: tiny organisms floating in the ocean.

poach: to catch or kill animals illegally.

GLOSSARY

pollen: a fine, yellow powder produced by flowering plants. Pollen is spread around by the wind, birds, and insects and is needed by a flower to make a seed.

pollination: transferring pollen from the male part of a flower to the female part so that the flower can make seeds.

pollinator: an insect or animal that moves pollen from plant to plant so new seeds can develop.

polyps: small creatures that live in colonies and form coral.

predator: an animal or plant that kills and eats other animals.

prey: an animal hunted and eaten by other animals.

producer: a part of the food chain that includes plants, which make their food through photosynthesis.

raptor: a bird of prey, such as an eagle, hawk, falcon, or owl, that hunts other animals.

refuge: a place that provides protection or safety.

regenerate: to form again, renewing or restoring something.

renewable energy: a form of energy that doesn't get used up, including the energy of the sun and the wind.

reproduction: making something new, just like itself.

reptile: a cold-blooded animal such as a snake, lizard, alligator, or turtle that has a spine, lays eggs, has scales or horny places, and breathes air.

resilient: describes the ability to recover quickly from setbacks.

riparian: related to the land at the edge of a stream, river, wetland, or other natural water source.

rodent: a mammal that uses its ever-growing front teeth to chew on things. Rodents make up more than half of all mammals on Earth and include mice, rats, squirrels, chipmunks, beavers, and gerbils.

sanctuary: a place of safety, where wildlife is protected.

scavenger: an animal, bird, or insect that eats rotting food or animals that are already dead.

sediment: bits of rock, sand, or dirt that have been carried to a place by water, wind, or a glacier.

seed dispersal: the spreading of seeds to new areas.

Serengeti: a vast grassland and woodland plains ecosystem in east-central Africa. In the Maasai language the name means "endless plains."

snare: a trap to catch wildlife.

sonication: the act of using sound to create vibrations to disrupt or shake something.

spawn: to produce and deposit eggs.

species: a group of organisms that share common traits and can reproduce offspring of their own kind.

squalene: a natural oil found in sharks and some plants that people use in medicine, cosmetics, and cleansers.

stereotype: an overly simple picture or opinion of a person, group, animal, or thing.

submersible: a boat that is designed to go completely underwater.

subtropical: related to an area near the tropics where the weather is warm.

sustainable: something that can be maintained at a certain level or rate.

sustainable tourism: tourism that minimizes negative effects on the environment or community by the people visiting a place.

taxidermist: a person who prepares, stuffs, and mounts the skins of animals to look lifelike.

temperate: not extreme in terms of climate or weather.

tourism: the business of people traveling for fun.

toxin: a poisonous or harmful substance.

Transcontinental Railroad: a railroad that spans North America from east to west.

trophic cascade: the changes that occur after a keystone species is gone that affect every species on every level of the food chain in an ecosystem.

tropical: the hot climate zone to the north and south of the equator.

tundra: the treeless area between the ice of the Arctic and the forests of northern lands.

ungulate: a hooved mammal.

urbanization: the process of becoming more like a city.

varroa mites: tiny parasites that attach themselves to bees and spread disease though a colony.

wallow: a depression in the ground, sometimes created by an animal, that holds water and allows animals to cool off, breed, drink, or relax.

watershed: an area of land that drains into a river or lake.

wetland: a low area filled with water, such as a marsh or swamp.

woody plant: a plant such as a shrub or tree that has hard stems and produces wood.

vegetation: all the plant life in a particular area.

vertebrate: an animal with a backbone.

zoology: the study of animals.

zooxanthellae: single-celled organisms that live inside coral polyps and other marine invertebrates.

Metric Conversions

Use this chart to find the metric equivalents to the English measurements in this book. If you need to know a half measurement, divide by two. If you need to know twice the measurement, multiply by two. How do you find a quarter measurement? How do you find three times the measurement?

English	Metric
1 inch	2.5 centimeters
1 foot	30.5 centimeters
1 yard	0.9 meter
1 mile	1.6 kilometers
1 pound	0.5 kilogram
1 teaspoon	5 milliliters
1 tablespoon	15 milliliters
1 cup	237 milliliters

ESSENTIAL QUESTIONS

Introduction: Why is it important to challenge scientific assumptions?

Chapter 1: How can understanding sharks help protect them?

Chapter 2: How did the disappearance of wolves in Yellowstone National Park affect its ecosystem?

Chapter 3: How do beavers transform ecosystems?

Chapter 4: How is the work of alligators important to their ecosystems?

Chapter 5: How do bees support biodiversity around the world?

Chapter 6: What would happen if a keystone mutualist such as the flying fox disappeared from its ecosystem?

Chapter 7: Why are the huge numbers of wildebeests and their Great Migration vital to the ecosystem of the East African plains?

Chapter 8: Why is it important to restore the bison to the North American Great Plains?

Chapter 9: Why are coral reefs sometimes called rainforests of the sea?

BOOKS

Castaldo, Nancy. *The Wolves and Moose of Isle Royale: Restoring an Island Ecosystem* (Scientists in the Field). Clarion Books, 2022.

Patent, Dorothy Hinshaw. *At Home with the Beaver: The Story of a Keystone Species*. Web of Life Children's Books, 2023.

Poliquin, Rachel. *Beavers: The Superpower Field Guide*. Clarion Books Reprint Edition, 2020.

Socha, Piotr. *Bees: A Honeyed History*. Abrams Books for Young Readers, 2017.

Spencer, Erin. *The World of Coral Reefs: Explore and Protect the Natural Wonders of the Sea*. Storey Publishing, 2022.

Stevens, Alison Pearce. *Animal Climate Heroes!* Godwin Books/Henry Holt and Company, 2024.

WEBSITES

American Museum of Natural History – Ology:
amnh.org/explore/ology

Center for Biological Diversity:
biologicaldiversity.org

Merlin Tuttle's Bat Conservation:
merlintuttle.org

National Geographic – Keystone Species:
education.nationalgeographic.org/resource/keystone-species

Role of Keystone Species in an Ecosystem:
education.nationalgeographic.org/resource/role-keystone-species-ecosystem/5th-grade

PBS – Climate and Our Planet:
nhpbs.pbslearningmedia.org/collection/climate-and-our-planet

San Diego Zoo Wildlife Alliance:
animals.sandiegozoo.org/animals

Smithsonian's National Museum of Natural History – Ocean:
ocean.si.edu

Smithsonian National Zoo & Conservation Biology Institute:
nationalzoo.si.edu/animals

The Bee Conservancy:
thebeeconservancy.org

RESOURCES

SELECT BIBLIOGRAPHY

bbc.com/future/article/20231120-wildebeest-and-wolves-a-secret-weapon-against-climate-change

biointeractive.org/classroom-resources/some-animals-are-more-equal-others-keystone-species-and-trophic-cascades

cincinnati-oh.gov/cincyparks/news/keystone-species-series-american-alligator

education.nationalgeographic.org/resource/role-keystone-species-ecosystem

fish.wa.gov.au/documents/recreational_fishing/fact_sheets/fact_sheet_whale_shark.pdf

fs.usda.gov/wildflowers/pollinators/pollinator-of-the-month/perdita_minima

graywolfconservation.com/Wild_Wolves/history.htm

nationalgeographic.com/animals/article/elephant-footprints-frog-habitat-ecosystem-engineers

nationalgeographic.com/animals/article/keystone-species

nationalzoo.si.edu/animals/american-bison

natura-pacific.com/wp-content/uploads/2019/10/Bats-First-Senior-resource-Flying-Foxes-why-they-are-important-SAMMEL.pdf

noaa.gov/education/resource-collections/climate/carbon-cycle

nps.gov/articles

nps.gov/articles/bison-bellows-10-6-

nrdc.org/stories/keystone-species-101

ocean.si.edu/ocean-life/sharks-rays/sharks

parks.canada.ca/pn-np/ab/elkisland/nature/eep-sar/ecologie-ecology2

pbs.org/wnet/nature/serengeti-rules-dhbtnm/19906

science.org/content/article/european-union-expands-ban-three-neonicotinoid-pesticides

smithsonianmag.com/science-nature/beavers-the-engineers-of-the-forest-11145929

true.travel/journal/great-migration-guide

worldwildlife.org

QR CODE GLOSSARY

Page 4: nhpbs.pbslearningmedia.org/resource/nat38-discovery-of-keystone-species-vid/the-serengeti-rules-media-gallery

Page 5: media.hhmi.org/biointeractive/click/keystone/index.html

Page 7: amnh.org/explore/ology/biodiversity/what-is-biodiversity

Page 14: ed.ted.com/lessons/why-are-sharks-so-awesome-tierney-thys

Page 15: visitcaymanislands.com/en-us/isdhf/isdhf-bios/dr-eugenie-clark

Page 16: climatekids.nasa.gov/climate-change-meaning

Page 17: ocean.si.edu/ocean-life/sharks-rays/sharks

Page 19: pewtrusts.org/en/research-and-analysis/data-visualizations/2012/infographic-sharks-count

Page 20: seafoodwatch.org

Page 21: envhumanities.sites.gettysburg.edu/es225b-spring19/public-perception-of-the-great-white-shark/ecological-importance-of-the-great-white-shark

Page 27: nps.gov/yell/learn/photosmultimedia/qa-wolves.htm

Page 31: education.nationalgeographic.org/resource/wolves-101

QR CODE GLOSSARY (CONT.)

Page 32: *wdfw.wa.gov/species-habitats/at-risk/species-recovery/gray-wolf/influence*

Page 37: *pbs.org/wnet/nature/leave-it-to-beavers-infographic-beavers-101/8868*

Page 37: *pbs.org/wnet/nature/leave-it-to-beavers-video-how-beavers-build-dams/8847*

Page 42: *youtube.com/watch?v=rpWKd9uT2Ro*

Page 47: *evergladesfoundation.org/post/9-amazing-things-you-didn-t-know-about-alligators*

Page 48: *evergladesfoundation.org/history*

Page 50: *kids.nationalgeographic.com/history/article/endangered-species-act*

Page 52: *everglades.org*

Page 53: *nps.gov/ever/learn/nature/habitats.htm*

Page 55: *nps.gov/ever/learn/photosmultimedia/dreaming-of-the-everglades-film.htm*

Page 59: *ed.ted.com/lessons/why-do-honeybees-love-hexagons-zack-patterson-and-andy-peterson*

Page 61: *wholekidsfoundation.org/inside-the-beehive*

Page 63: *thebeeconservancy.org/10-ways-to-save-the-bees*

Page 63: *thebeeconservancy.org/citizen-community-science-for-bees*

Page 64: *un.org/en/observances/bee-day#:~:text=To%20raise%20awareness%20of%20the,May%20as%20World%20Bee%20Day*

Page 71: *sydneybats.org.au/education/bat-videos/no-tree-no-me*

Page 73: *sydneybats.org.au/education/bats4kids*

Page 74: *ausbats.org.au/our-bats.html*

Page 76: *batcon.org/about-bats/bats-101/?gclid=CjwKCAjw7oeqBhBwEiwALyHLM0P-ysiC5FZv6FyXkCuqQmuLDqZNFXp3-af2KIJc59NyhVTOGpkASRoC-_cQAvD_BwE*

Page 78: *classroompoems.com/how-to-write-an-ode.html*

Page 81: *awf.org/wildlife-conservation/wildebeest*

Page 83: *youtube.com/watch?v=oTw4XnLnSmU*

Page 84: *pbs.org/video/wildebeest-cross-crocodile-infested-water*

Page 88: *expertafrica.com/tanzania/info/serengeti-wildebeest-migration*

Page 95: *explore.org/search/bison*

Page 97: *treehugger.com/difference-between-bison-and-buffalo-6499776*

Page 98: *siarchives.si.edu/history/featured-topics/stories/william-temple-hornaday-saving-american-bison/image-gallery-william-temple-hornaday*

Page 103: *rmg.co.uk/stories/topics/what-coral*

Page 104: *nhm.ac.uk/discover/quick-questions/why-are-coral-reefs-important.html*

Page 105: *oceanservice.noaa.gov/facts/coralreef-climate.html*

Page 107: *oceanservice.noaa.gov/podcast/sep15/os11-bleaching.html*

Page 108: *oceanservice.noaa.gov/facts/thingsyoucando.html*

Page 110: *education.nationalgeographic.org/resource/saving-ocean-biodiversity-coral-restoration*

Page 111: *reasonstobecheerful.world/coral-reefs-healthy-noise*

Page 112: *oceanservice.noaa.gov/facts/acidification.html*

INDEX

F

Fairfax, Emily, 41
flying foxes, 68–79
  overview of, 68
  conservation of, 75–76, 79
  in food chain, 68–70, 72
  habitats of, 68, 71–72, 74–76
  roles of, 69–70
  sense of sight of, 73
  threats to, 71–74
food chain/food web
  alligators in, 45–46, 48–49, 51
  beavers in, 27, 37, 39, 42
  bees in, 58–66
  bison in, 90–94, 99–100
  corals in, 101, 103, 105, 109
  flying foxes in, 68–70, 72
  keystone species in, 2–4, 6, 8, 11
  sharks in, 13–15, 19
  wildebeests in, 81–83
  wolves in, 25–28, 31–32, 34
forest elephants, 86
foundational species, 8, 103

G

gray wolves. *See* wolves
green-backed firecrowns, 59

H

Haaland, Deb, 97
herbivores, 2–3, 81, 86, 90
Hornaday, William Temple, 96–97, 98
human threats
  to alligators, 49–51, 53
  to beavers, 39–41
  to bees, 61–63
  to bison, 94–96
  conservation to counter. *See* conservation
  to corals, 105–107, 112–113
  to flying foxes, 71–74
  hyperkeystone species and, 8–9
  to sharks, 17–18
  to wildebeests, 84, 87
  to wolves, 28–29, 31
hyperkeystone species, 8–9

K

Kahumbu, Paula, 83
keystone species
  alligators as, 45–56
  beavers as, 27, 35–44
  bees as, 57–67
  bison as, 31, 90–100
  corals as, 14, 19, 101–113
  definition of, 1–2
  disappearance or removal of, 4–6
  flying foxes as, 68–79
  locations of, iv–v, 7, 10
  research on, 2–9
  sharks as, 12–24
  types of, 8
  wildebeests as, 80–89
  wolves as, 25–34
krill, 8

L

Leopold, Aldo, 30

M

mutualists, 8, 58, 59, 68, 79

N

Native Americans, 28, 94–95, 97, 98
Nedimyer, Ken, 107

P

Paine, Robert, 3–5, 7, 8, 29
parrotfish, 109
peccaries, 47
pollination, 58–61, 62, 64–67, 70
Pope, Lawrence, 75
prairie dogs, 93
predators, 2–4, 12, 14, 25, 32, 34, 45–46

S

saguaro cacti, 11
seagrass, 15, 17, 24
seed dispersal, 69–70, 71, 86, 93, 100

sharks, 12–24
  overview of, 12–13
  climate change and, 15–17
  conservation of, 18, 19–21
  in food chain, 13–15, 19
  habitats of, 13, 23
  hunting of, 17–18
  role of, 14–15
sight, sense of, 73, 77
Sinclair, Tony, 81, 85
smell, sense of, 34, 62
Smith, Doug, 27
starfish, purple, 4, 7, 12

T

termites, 38
tidepools, 3–5
trophic cascades, 6, 26, 104

W

wallows, 47–48, 56, 94
wildebeests, 80–89
  overview of, 80–81
  conservation of, 85–87
  in food chain, 81–83
  habitats of, 80–82, 84, 86
  migration of, 82–88
  role of, 81–82
  threats to, 81, 83–84
wolves, 25–34
  overview of, 25
  attitudes toward, 25, 29–30, 32–33
  communication by, 27, 29
  conservation of, 29–32
  family structure of, 28, 29
  in food chain, 25–28, 31–32, 34
  habitats of, 25
  threats to, 28–29
  in Yellowstone, 27, 29, 30–32

Y

Yellowstone National Park, 27, 29, 30–32, 95, 98